T0285124

THE FUTURE

CONNOR BEDARD AND THE CHICAGO BLACKHAWKS' NEW ERA

TAB BAMFORD

TRIUMPH
BOOKS

No part of this publication may be reproduced, stored in a retrieval system, or transmitted in any form by any means, electronic, mechanical, photocopying, or otherwise, without the prior written permission of the publisher, Triumph Books LLC, 814 North Franklin Street, Chicago, Illinois 60610.

Library of Congress Cataloging-in-Publication Data available upon request.

This book is available in quantity at special discounts for your group or organization. For further information, contact:

Triumph Books LLC
814 North Franklin Street
Chicago, Illinois 60610
(312) 337-0747
www.triumphbooks.com

Printed in U.S.A.
ISBN: 978-1-63727-703-4
Design and page production by Nord Compo

CONTENTS

CHAPTER 1

FALLING TO RISE

O N THE NIGHT OF THURSDAY, April 13, 2023, a book closed. It was a surreal night at the United Center on Chicago's West Side. In front of a packed house of 20,219 fans, the Chicago Blackhawks lost 5–4 to the Philadelphia Flyers in a game that meant absolutely nothing to either team in the chase for the playoffs.

Indeed, on this night, many fans of the two teams were more concerned with how the outcome would impact lottery balls and draft odds than with cheering for their team to actually win a game.

The Blackhawks came into the final game of their 2022–23 season having successfully knocked Sidney Crosby and the Pittsburgh Penguins out of the playoffs earlier in the week. That win cost the Blackhawks a chance to have the worst record in the NHL—and the best odds of winning the 2023 NHL Draft Lottery. The immediate gratification of beating a team like the Penguins was diluted by the angst that Chicago may have cost itself a chance at drafting the next great superstar.

That was the ironic scene set forth for that season finale. After a dramatic overtime period ended with a goal from

Philadelphia defenseman Ivan Provorov, the fans in Chicago stood. Many wiped away tears. And they applauded. Not because the Blackhawks had finished with the third-worst record in the entire league. But because this was the final game in a Blackhawks sweater for legendary center Jonathan Toews.

Earlier that morning, in a somewhat surprising move, Blackhawks general manager Kyle Davidson had held his season-ending media availability. He announced that the team would not be offering Toews another contract during the coming summer. The longest-tenured captain in the history of the Original Six franchise's time with the team was coming to an abrupt end.

With only hours' notice, fans bought up every available ticket for the game that night. When Toews stepped on the ice to warm up, he was greeted with a rousing ovation. When he scored a power play goal in the second period—what would be his final goal with the team—the ovation was at a level that hadn't been heard at the United Center in almost half a decade.

During the overtime period that night, Toews got a breakaway and almost ended the game. His shot was stopped, and the Flyers quickly ended the game with the Provorov goal. Close, but not quite.

As the Flyers congratulated their goaltender and began skating toward their bench to end their regular season, the Blackhawks began showing a Toews tribute video. It included highlights spanning the brilliant 15-year career of one of the faces of the resurrection of the Blackhawks franchise. One of those highlights was NHL commissioner Gary Bettman handing the Stanley Cup to Toews in Philadelphia 13 years earlier when he and his teammates ended the franchise's 49-year championship drought.

On an overtime goal. From Patrick Kane.

Kane and Toews joined the Blackhawks at the start of the 2007–08 season and were immediately tied together in the history of the organization. They were the odd couple of hockey royalty; Kane was a young guy who liked to have a good time while Toews was "Captain Serious." Kane scored the highlight-reel goals and had his trademark "Heartbreaker" celebration; Toews was stoic on a nightly basis, most times trying to shut down the opposition's best offensive threat.

Over the course of their careers, during which they had identical contracts, the two had only worn a single sweater— the Chicago Blackhawks'. Kane was the first No. 1 overall pick in franchise history, selected the year after Toews was drafted third. When they arrived, for the first time in years, the few remaining Blackhawks fans had hope for success.

Only a few weeks before their rookie seasons began, the Blackhawks organization was rocked by the passing of its principal owner, Bill Wirtz. Throughout that year, Kane and Toews wore jerseys with a WWW patch on their right shoulders in honor of the longtime owner.

That patch, and the passing of Bill Wirtz, was the precipice of another transition in the history of the Chicago Blackhawks. His son, Rocky, took control of the team—a team that had been called the worst-run organization in all of North American professional sports by ESPN and Forbes in the years before Bill's passing.

Rocky inherited a team that wasn't on local television and hadn't seen a playoff game in half a decade. Over the course of the previous 15 years, the Blackhawks had traded away franchise icons and fan favorites like Steve Larmer, Jeremy Roenick, Ed Belfour, and Chris Chelios.

The only thing worse than angry fans is apathetic fans. And, frankly, Chicago simply did not care about the Chicago Blackhawks.

During the 2006–07 season—the year before Kane and Toews arrived—the Blackhawks finished second-to-last in average attendance in the NHL. In one of the largest arenas in the league with a capacity around 20,000 for home games, Chicago drew only 12,727 per night. The only team worse than Chicago that season was the rival St. Louis Blues.

There were nights you could show up with an expired student ID an hour before puck drop and get in for $15. And, if the Blackhawks were playing a team against which they had a history, like the Detroit Red Wings, the overwhelming majority of the fans in the seats would be cheering for the wrong team.

What had once been an incredible hockey city was in need of a spark. Change was desperately needed in every way. And Rocky Wirtz was the right man at the right time to lead organizational changes while Kane and Toews brought a pulse to the on-ice product.

The Blackhawks were still struggling to get past the idea they were "cheap" with agents around the league. They had to admittedly overpay for free agents Brian Campbell and Cristobal Huet in 2008 just to get agents to answer their phones when calling from a 312 area code. But the times were quickly changing in Chicago, even if the rest of the hockey world was slow to recognize it.

When the Blackhawks hosted the Red Wings at Wrigley Field in the Winter Classic on New Year's Day in 2009, it was a coming-out party of sorts for the young lineup. Defensemen Duncan Keith and Brent Seabrook had developed into one of the best tandems in the league, and the Blackhawks had some young skill surrounding Kane and Toews. Patrick Sharp, Dustin Byfuglien, Dave Bolland, and Kris Versteeg were starting to see their last names on jerseys at home games. And there were more than a handful of fans walking the concourses at the United Center.

After a first trip to the playoffs with their young team ended at the hands of the Red Wings in the Western Conference Final that spring, there was reason to believe the Blackhawks were ascending. They were dangerous.

The addition of free-agent forward Marian Hossa made the hockey world take them seriously.

In the six seasons that followed Hossa's arrival, the Blackhawks won three championships—doubling the number of banners hanging from the rafters above their home ice. Toews, Kane, and Keith were each awarded the Conn Smythe Trophy after the three championships.

During the run, fans watched as Toews and Keith won multiple gold medals with Canada at the Winter Olympics. In 2010, before the first Stanley Cup championship, Red Wings coach Mike Babcock—who was coaching a stacked Canada roster—said his best line was "whatever line Jonathan Toews is on." He was a stud. And Canada needed him to play well in the gold-medal game, in which they beat Kane and the United States.

The National Hockey League recognized the Blackhawks were good for leaguewide business too. It felt like every year

the Blackhawks played in one of the league's signature outdoor games. They played at Soldier Field and in South Bend,
Indiana, on Notre Dame's football field. The United Center
hosted the Frozen Four. It was an incredible time to be a
Blackhawks fan.

But the clock is undefeated—as is the NHL's hard salary
cap. As the years went by, the Blackhawks didn't replenish
their roster around their stars as well. Playoff runs lasted
fewer games. And soon, the playoffs were no longer in the
picture.

Kane and Toews got older, like everyone does. They still
played at a high level, but they weren't able to carry the team
every night. With the supporting cast struggling and players
leaving to get paid elsewhere because of the salary cap limits,
the Blackhawks were no longer the shining beacon in the
league they once had been.

On November 6, 2018, the Blackhawks announced they
had fired the most successful head coach in franchise history.
After a great run of 10-plus seasons behind the bench, Joel
Quenneville was out. He was replaced by a relative unknown
named Jeremy Colliton, who was greeted with skepticism by
most fans.

The United Center was still packed most nights, however.
Until the COVID-19 pandemic brought the entire sports
world to a frozen stop in March of 2020, the Blackhawks
had sold out every game since March 8, 2008.

The stoppage that occurred during the pandemic started
seismic changes in the Blackhawks organization that climaxed
with Toews' final home game three years later.

Team president John McDonough was surprisingly fired on
April 27, 2020—just weeks after play had paused indefinitely.

At the time, with limited media access because of the pandemic, there were lots of questions about the departure that went unanswered.

When the NHL opened back up in two bubbles for a rewritten playoff format in Toronto and Edmonton, the Blackhawks barely qualified to take the ice. They upset the Edmonton Oilers before having one of the most awkward, frustrating seasons in franchise history come to an end.

The coming months led to more struggles for the Blackhawks. Toews announced shortly before the abbreviated 2021 season that he was opting to not play the entire year. He needed to focus on his health. Over the years, Chicago's captain had dealt with serious concussion symptoms and played through a series of injuries. He shared later that he had Chronic Inflammatory Response Syndrome (CIRS), a by-product of having a bad case of COVID during the time the NHL was shut down.

There were whispers that Kane was playing through some physical limitations of his own as well. Though he consistently denied anything being wrong, there were times that he didn't quite have the same jump that brought fans out of their seats.

October 2021 changed everything for the franchise.

The team's 535-game sellout streak at the United Center came to an end on October 24, 2021. Fans were starting to walk away with the team struggling on the ice amidst rumors that there was a pending lawsuit. They were still buying their No. 19 and No. 88 jerseys, but not as many were buying tickets to watch them play in person.

Four days after the sellout streak ended, former forward prospect Kyle Beach came forward and put his name on a report of sexual assault that had been covered up by the organization in 2010. The news rocked the hockey landscape and the Chicago Blackhawks, who retained Jenner & Block LLP to conduct an investigation into Beach's claims. The report was provided to the Blackhawks' ownership group on October 26, 2021, and led to the immediate dismissal of general manager Stan Bowman. Soon thereafter, Quenneville resigned from his job with the Florida Panthers.

The once-great dynasty teams were permanently tarnished.

The wake of the Jenner & Block report led to massive changes off the ice for the Blackhawks. Rocky's son, Danny, became a more visible part of the leadership group. With Bowman gone, the Blackhawks named Kyle Davidson the interim general manager and began a search for a permanent replacement.

Toews returned for the 2021–22 season, but he was a shell of his former self. He appeared in 71 games and scored only 12 goals, the worst season of his pro career.

On the third anniversary of Quenneville's firing, the Blackhawks parted ways with his successor. Colliton was fired and replaced by Derek King, who had been the head coach of the team's AHL affiliate in Rockford. The first significant move of Davidson's tenure as the team's GM was changing head coaches. It wouldn't be the last.

Before that season, Bowman had made a strong push to add veteran pieces to make another playoff run. The 1–9–2 start to the season that cost Colliton his job also made it painfully obvious that the playoffs weren't in the cards. With the blessing of the Wirtz family, Davidson started to aggressively make changes to his NHL roster.

On March 1, 2022, Kyle Davidson was named the permanent general manager of the Blackhawks. Just weeks before the NHL's trade deadline, he went to work gutting his team to begin an aggressive rebuild. Davidson traded future Hall of Fame goaltender Marc-André Fleury, who was acquired from Vegas before the season, for draft picks. He also traded one of the team's few young bright spots, Brandon Hagel, to the Tampa Bay Lightning for a package of picks and players. It was a fire sale in Chicago.

The trade deadline didn't end the exodus from the roster. During the summer of 2022, Davidson allowed forwards Dylan Strome and Dominik Kubalik to leave as free agents. He then shocked the league just before the 2022 draft when he traded star forward Alex DeBrincat to the Ottawa Senators and center Kirby Dach, who had been the third overall pick just three years prior, to the Montreal Canadiens.

Davidson had the green light to chart a new path for the franchise, and that included a clean slate. On opening night of the 2022–23 season, the only players remaining from the dynasty teams were Jonathan Toews and Patrick Kane.

Given the direction of the franchise, both players faced relentless questions throughout training camp and early in the season about being traded. What was once unthinkable was now a very real possibility. Both did their best to limit their comments and efforts to their performance on the ice, but you could tell the questions—and the anxiety that came from potentially making a life-altering decision—were weighing on them.

Then, in late December, Toews missed a couple games because of an illness. In January, he acknowledged that he needed to take a step back from the game to get his body right once again. When—if—he returned to the lineup was up in the air, and his trade potential was gone.

But Kane was still in the room. He joked at times that it would be nice if Toews were around to answer the trade-related questions with him. The first time Kane showed some frustration with the process was when the New York Rangers traded for Blues forward Vladimir Tarasenko.

By virtue of his no-trade clause, Kane could effectively select his ultimate destination if he were open to leaving Chicago. There were reports that the Rangers were one of the few teams that interested him; his former linemate, Artemi Panarin, was skating there. Kane won the Hart Memorial Trophy as the league's Most Valuable Player with Panarin on the opposite wing and the two remained close. So, when the Rangers acquired another right wing, Kane wasn't happy.

The injury whispers had now become open conversations. But Kane put some of that to rest with a hot streak before the deadline that made him an attractive asset once again. And he got his wish: Davidson facilitated a trade to the Rangers before the trade deadline.

Which brings us back to the night of April 13.

After not playing for two full months, Toews returned from his illness on April 1. He appeared in seven games to close the regular season, four of which were on the road.

While the tribute video played, the Flyers team stayed on their bench. Never one to chase the limelight, Toews did his best to not lose his composure during the video. As it came to a close, both teams tapped their sticks on the ice and the boards in recognition of the tremendous career of Chicago's captain. In a Blackhawks hat, he skated around the ice and waved to the fans who had adored him for nearly two decades.

His time in Chicago was over. Kane was gone as well.

The dynasty era was officially over.

The Blackhawks were moving on to the next.

———————

On November 16, 2018—less than two weeks after the Blackhawks fired Joel Quenneville—*The Hockey News* published a cover story that got everyone's attention. Senior writer Ken Campbell wrote a piece titled "Meet the Future of Hockey, 13-Year-Old Connor Bedard."

That article introduced us to a "young man who is inviting comparison to the likes of Sidney Crosby and Connor McDavid, and has the work ethic to match." Even though he was playing against players years older than him, Bedard was putting up video game numbers already. There was a buzz growing around a player who was three years away from driving a car—and five years away from being eligible for the NHL draft.

The years that followed did nothing to slow the hype around the young player who was becoming a bit of an urban legend in western Canada.

As a 14-year-old, Bedard was granted special status to play on West Van's U-18 team; he was playing against players as much as four years his senior. Other great players from the area like Mathew Barzal and Ryan Nugent-Hopkins had not received that level of exemption.

He became just the seventh player ever to earn "exceptional" status to play at the top level of Canadian Junior Hockey. He later shared that Wayne Gretzky called to congratulate him. Bedard joined the Regina Pats in the WHL as a 15-year-old after gaining that status from the league. Skating against players who were up to 20 years old at the time, Bedard produced 28 points in 15 games.

In his first full season in the WHL, Bedard showed that he was becoming a game-changing player. He scored 51 goals and added 49 assists in 62 games as a 16-year-old. The word *phenom* felt too light when speaking about the record-breaking accomplishments he was stacking up on the ice already at such a young age.

As media outlets in Canada and the United States started to shift their focus to the 2022 NHL Draft, the conversation inevitably moved to the following year. There were a few prospects at the top of the class, including Bedard, who most onlookers felt were better than anyone in the 2022 group.

Everyone was thinking about the 2023 NHL Draft already.

The 2022 World Junior Championship was the first time an international audience got to see Bedard play against the best under-20 players from around the globe. Though the tournament was pushed to August because of a COVID outbreak in December, that didn't keep Bedard from making an impact despite being three years younger than many of the players he was competing against. He had eight points in seven games and was one of the better players on Canada's gold-medal-winning squad.

Dennis Williams served as an assistant coach in 2022 and was then tasked with serving as the head coach for the Hockey Canada 2023 World Junior Championship team. When COVID delayed the 2022 version until late summer, it made the gap between tournaments smaller—which made the job of the coaches putting together two rosters of eligible players a bit trickier. But Williams knew Bedard would be an important player in the 2023 tournament after his strong performance over the summer.

"For him being a part of that first one when we had the start in Edmonton and then finish off the summer because that was postponed because of COVID…there were a lot of good lessons learned for him in that event because he was the youngest still by far," Williams recalled. "At [the 2022] tournament, he was penciled in more in a depth role as a 13th-, 12th-type forward to start. And I remember the coaches having discussions about his ability to play and his skill level. When you're playing against 19-year-olds [as a 16-year-old], that's a hard event to play at.

"But it didn't take long for him to move up the lineup quickly in that event. And then when he came back in the [2023 World Juniors] in Halifax, you could just see how determined he was."

Williams was familiar with Bedard's abilities, unfortunately, as the head coach of the Everett Silvertips—a team that also competes in the Western Hockey League. Scouting Bedard as an opponent was nearly impossible because of his awareness on the ice, Williams said. He could force the defense to commit and then make a play for a teammate, or rip one of his patented shots on net and beat even the best game plans with his own skill.

Having Bedard on his side for the World Juniors gave Williams and his staff confidence they could win.

Bedard returned to Regina and continued to tear up the WHL. In December, the regularly scheduled World Junior Championship tournament came around again. Bedard was nearly unstoppable. Every game he produced a highlight that took fans' breath away. Every night he had an impact on the box score. And after every game, when he was asked about his personal performance, Bedard deflected the praise to his teammates.

That humility stood out to his coaches in the tournament.

"I remember when I called him when the team was made and he was like, 'Let's get another one,'" Williams remembered. "When you look back at what he said after the final game—where I don't think he had a point—it was all about the team. Throughout the tournament, Connor deflected all the press the best he could because he's such a good team guy. Even though he wasn't in our leadership group, guys definitely looked up to him despite his age."

He was named the Most Valuable Player in the tournament after scoring nine goals with 14 assists in just seven games. Canada won gold for the second time in six months—both times with Bedard being one of the better offensive players in the entire tournament. His production put him on the top of television graphics that included the names of Gretzky, Jaromír Jágr, and Eric Lindros—all-time greats who will all be in the Hockey Hall of Fame in Toronto (if Jágr ever retires). His tournament was so dominant that the IIHF named Bedard its Male Player of the Year in June, beating out established NHL veterans for the honor.

"I've been going to that tournament for more than two decades," one NHL scout told ESPN's Emily Kaplan before the draft. "And what Connor Bedard did, especially with all of the attention and eyes on him, is as impressive of an individual performance as you'll ever see. The only way I can describe it is pure dominance."

If hockey had a phenomenon comparable to the Beatles in the 1960s or Michael Jackson in the 1980s, Bedard was it.

Crowds started following him wherever he went. His Regina team played in front of a sold-out crowd of 17,000-plus at the Saddledome in Calgary (home of the Flames). He was terrific on the ice and even better at the box office. Connor Bedard was great for hockey business.

Brad Herauf became an assistant coach with the Regina Pats in 2015, well before Bedard arrived on the scene. But he was blown away by the impact Bedard had on the local economy and the Western Hockey League as a whole.

"On a business level, the dollars he drove for the league were astronomical. I think the attendance and the revenue he drove not just for the Regina Pats, but for the whole WHL league in every market, I think is something we have never seen before."

Herauf became the head coach in Regina following John Paddock's retirement after Bedard's final season. If the impact Bedard made was impressive on the league, he left an indelible mark on the Regina franchise and Herauf as well.

"But personally, for me, he's made me think about myself and the way I am with my career," Herauf said. "I think Connor's one of the people that's truly striving to be the best version of himself. He's truly driven in one line, into wanting to be this thing. He inspired a lot of kids—the younger minor hockey kids—which is super important. But for our group, Connor left a work ethic and a process in place in which he was the first guy to show up and the last guy to leave. And that's how we want all of our lead hockey players to be here; everybody—it doesn't matter if you're the best player or worst player.

"We want the kind of guys who will work hard and to do whatever they can to maximize themselves. Something Connor said to me one time—and he's not a selfish player whatsoever, he is not a selfish teammate whatsoever—but he did say to me one time about his own development, 'Brad, hockey players have to be selfish with their development.' And I think it is one of the most intelligent things I've ever heard because I don't think a lot of hockey players take enough onus and responsibility on making sure that they're the best version of themselves.

"Sometimes they just wait for their coaches or their trainers in the off-season to make them better. Connor's someone that every day is actively seeking out ways to be better, how would he become a better hockey player? And that's why I say he's a self-made person. He has the talent, but he has the work ethic that goes with that eliteness."

After all of the accolades, awards, individual highlights, and team successes with Regina and Hockey Canada, the next step was something fans had been anticipating for years. Hockey fans across the globe had Monday, May 8, 2023, circled on their calendar from the moment the NHL announced that was when the league's draft lottery would be held.

Scouts, media members, analysts, and fans had all been talking up a 5'10" center in western Canada, and that would be the night one team's fortunes would change.

As the broadcast of the draft lottery played out, there were conversations on the sets in Canada and the United States about the depth of the draft. Adam Fantilli was having a record-breaking freshman season at the University of Michigan. Leo Carlsson had also shown very well at the World Juniors for Sweden. Will Smith had emerged as a legitimate top-five pick with his strong play for the United States Development Program. And Russian forward Matvei Michkov, who hadn't been able to play in either of the previous two World Junior Championships because of an IIHF ban of Russian teams, was a wild card because of his contract in the KHL.

But everyone wanted No. 1. There was no question who would go first.

When NHL Deputy Commissioner Bill Daly flipped over the card showing the Chicago Blackhawks had won the draft lottery for only the second time in team history, the party at the United Center exploded with cheering and applause. Living rooms all over Chicago saw hockey fans exchanging high fives and hugs.

Connor Bedard was going to be a Chicago Blackhawk.

At Wrigley Field, where the Cubs were playing that night, the video boards showed the Blackhawks had won the lottery. The PA played the Blackhawks' signature goal song, "Chelsea Dagger" by The Fratellis, to a huge ovation. The White Sox were on the road in Kansas City, and the players were so excited in the dugout that it was mentioned during their broadcast. The entire city was excited.

And the "good for business" label followed Bedard to Chicago—even if he wouldn't officially be drafted until June 28. When fans woke up the morning after the draft lottery, many had already spent money to see him play in person. The Blackhawks sold more than 500 full season ticket packages and grossed $5.2 million in ticketing revenue in less than a day following the draft lottery.

As he always did, Bedard deflected questions leading up to the draft. He never assumed he would be the first overall pick, even if every general manager, prospect, head coach, television analyst, and fan knew better. He always just limited his answers to "If they pick me" or "It would be an honor to be selected first."

The only outstanding question leading up to the draft was whether Bedard would wear his customary No. 98, which he had for Regina, or 16, which he wore for Canada at the World Juniors. The Blackhawks and the NHL couldn't officially sell his name on a jersey before he was drafted and signed his contract, but that didn't stop Chicago fans from custom ordering their own. And they did it in droves.

When Bedard arrived in Nashville in late June for the draft, even he couldn't ignore the sea of red and white Blackhawks jerseys with his name and No. 98 on the back. Chicago fans showed up in droves; the Blackhawks hosted watch parties in Chicago and Nashville for the night of the first round of the draft. And they were both packed with fans eagerly anticipating the moment Bedard would officially become a Blackhawk.

Always a loyal player, Bedard spent his draft day getting ready with his family and had lunch with a number of members of the Regina Pats organization who made the trip to Nashville to see him selected.

Standard practice at the draft is for players to join the members of the organization on hand and put on a team jersey for a photo opportunity on the stage after their name is called. The number on the jerseys the players receive is usually the year; the other 31 players selected in the first round of the 2023 NHL Draft had their pictures taken in No. 23 jerseys. Not Bedard.

With the first overall selection in the 2023 NHL Draft, the Chicago Blackhawks are very proud to select, from the Regina Pats of the Western Hockey League, Connor Bedard.

When Bedard joined Kyle Davidson; Danny Wirtz; head coach Luke Richardson; and other members of the Blackhawks' front office, business operations, and scouting staffs, he was handed the iconic red Blackhawks sweater. The number on the sleeves and back: 98. Once again, Bedard received "exceptional status" and got his number of choice from the first time he put on an NHL sweater.

In Chicago, Bedard jerseys went on sale moments after his name was called at the Blackhawks' watch party. The line was almost around the block to buy one immediately.

On July 4, Sportico published an episode of its *Sporticast* podcast featuring an interview with Blackhawks president of business operations Jaime Faulkner. This was less than one week after the NHL draft, but the sports business world was obsessed with how Bedard was selling already in Chicago.

"You know what's interesting, I think if you're in the hockey world you know who Connor Bedard is," Faulkner told the hosts. "If you're a general sports fan, there has been enough hype about him that if you are a sports fan, you are aware of who he is. You might not know the full extent of why he's so popular, but you know enough to say, 'He's the next Connor McDavid. He's being compared to Wayne Gretzky.'"

Faulkner went on to say she had traveled to London, where the Chicago Cubs were playing the St. Louis Cardinals in a marquee Major League Baseball event during the 2023 season, and there was buzz there about Bedard.

As of the time of that interview, Faulkner said the Blackhawks had more than 90 percent of their existing season ticket holders renew and more than 3,000 new season ticket packages sold—and they were excluding brokers from their numbers. Selecting Bedard was worth "multiple millions of dollars" in the first week after the draft, according to Faulkner.

Not only that, the Blackhawks' social media engagement for their sixth- and seventh-round picks in the 2023 NHL Draft was better than the numbers drawn by the posts from Anaheim and Columbus for the second and third overall picks in the draft. The trickle-down was enormous for everything Chicago Blackhawks.

The first chance Blackhawks fans could have had to see Bedard was immediately following the draft. The day after the conclusion of the selection process, the Blackhawks flew all of their new prospects (who were available) to Chicago to join some other previously drafted players for their annual development camp.

This year, however, the Blackhawks opted not to have any on-ice workouts. The week wasn't open to the public like usual; instead, the team had their players working out together, going through team-build exercises, and getting to know the city of Chicago. Among the tasks placed upon Bedard: throwing out the first pitch at a Cubs game that was attended by the full collection of Blackhawks prospects.

That did not slow down the hype around Bedard. Rapper Drake announced that his new tour would begin in Chicago during that week with an image of Bedard on his Instagram account. And there were fans lined up around the Blackhawks' practice facility hoping for a glimpse—or even an autograph—of the new star in town.

Even without ever getting on the ice, Bedard impressed his potential future teammates during the development camp. Frank Nazar, one of the Blackhawks' first-round picks in 2022, who was heading back to play his sophomore season at the University of Michigan—where he was a teammate of No. 3 overall pick Adam Fantilli the previous year—was impressed by Bedard's humility.

"I thought he was a super cool guy," Nazar said. "Just getting to know him just a little bit while I was there and kind of understand him a bit and just seeing how humble he is…. A man that's that famous and that popular, just walking around just like another kid is really cool to see. Just how he didn't show off to anyone or one-up anyone and trying to think he was better than anyone and that was really cool to see from him. And I was happy to see that."

Landon Slaggert was one of the older prospects at the development camp. A Chicago pick in 2020, he opted to return for a senior season at Notre Dame instead of signing with the Blackhawks. He would later be named the captain of the Fighting Irish for his final collegiate season. Bedard's commitment to the game was something that he took away from their time together.

"Getting to meet him at development camp, he's a high-character kid and obviously someone you want to be around," Slaggert said. "He's so locked in and cares for the game so much. It was impressive just to see him in the short time that I did at development camp."

Among the list of things he had on his schedule, Bedard met with the Chicago media twice during that week. He had already signed endorsement deals with Upper Deck for memorabilia and Lululemon for clothing. The most important contract he signed was with the Blackhawks, which the team officially announced on his 18th birthday—July 17.

After the whirlwind week in Chicago, life returned to somewhat normal. Bedard went back to training and the Chicago sports scene turned more of its attention to the two baseball teams in town and the start of Bears training camp.

There was still talk about Bedard coming, but his formal arrival wouldn't happen until September, when the Blackhawks opened their training camp.

Unfortunately, for all of the transitions in the preceding months for the Chicago Blackhawks as an organization, there was one that came unexpectedly in late July. Rocky Wirtz, the chairman of the club, died suddenly after a brief illness.

Just as his father hadn't seen Kane and Toews on the ice, Rocky would never get a chance to see the next generation of Blackhawks begin with Bedard. And, just as Kane and Toews had in their rookie seasons, Bedard would wear a patch on his jersey for every game of his rookie season honoring the team's late owner. This time, it would be a black circle that read "ROCKY."

On August 8, the Wirtz family held a private funeral service for Rocky. Many of the players from the championship seasons attended, including Toews and Kane. They were joined by some of the living legends of the franchise like Denis Savard and Chris Chelios. Connor Bedard also attended the service, showing his understanding of the impact Rocky had on the franchise as well as what his individual place is in the future of the franchise.

In only a few short weeks, Bedard would take the ice with his new teammates in Chicago. His summer was flying by. For hockey fans, it wasn't moving fast enough. Chicago wanted to see Connor Bedard play. And the time was coming for the next era of Blackhawks hockey to begin.

CHAPTER 2

"I LIKE HOCKEY"

"I HAVEN'T PLAYED A GAME in a long time and that's what I want to do. I'm a rookie like any other guy here.… I want to play a game so bad; it's been so long. So I'm really excited for that."

On September 13, the Blackhawks prospects took to the ice together to get ready for the Tom Kurvers Prospect Showcase in Minnesota. Chicago's prospects would play two games, first against the St. Louis Blues' prospects on Saturday evening and then against the Minnesota Wild's prospects on Sunday afternoon.

The collection of players on the ice on that beautiful Wednesday in Chicago included a number of former first-round picks and many of the other top young players in the organization. Each of them was looking to make their mark and impress the coaches and front office. And they got a chance to do it for one day without Connor Bedard on the ice.

Bedard was finishing up a whirlwind conclusion of his summer in Las Vegas at the NHL's North American players media tour. He was there representing the Blackhawks with veteran Seth Jones. For the first time in public, he was being treated as the face of the franchise.

That event came after Bedard made fans wander around Instagram looking for videos of him working out in Toronto and then at the NHLPA/Upper Deck Rookie Showcase in Arlington, Virginia. There, Bedard and Kevin Korchinski were the two Blackhawks prospects who got their pictures taken for their first hockey cards from Upper Deck.

Bedard also attended the BioSteel Camp with other NHL superstars like Connor McDavid, Leon Draisaitl, Nathan MacKinnon, and Cale Makar. The elite of the elite were together for a few days working out in the gym and on the ice, collectively getting ready for the coming season.

"It's great to be on the ice and see what they do, see little moves or what plays they're making, and you can learn a lot just kind of watching those guys," Bedard said when he finally arrived in Chicago. "I think every shift, every game you can learn something. [It's] the same approach when you're with them in a practice environment."

Bedard joined the rest of the Blackhawks' prospects on Thursday, September 14—just hours after the parent company of BioSteel, one of his sponsors, filed for bankruptcy protection in Canada and the United States. He wasn't worried about a potential loss of endorsement income, though. He was focused on hitting the ice with his future teammates.

Leading up to his arrival, there were questions about whether it made sense for the Blackhawks to even skate him in a prospect showcase. That's usually a weekend reserved for players who will go back to junior and spend the coming year in the AHL. But every time he was asked about it, Bedard's response was as consistent as it had been since he answered questions during the Blackhawks' development camp in July.

He just wanted to be one of the guys.

Being one of the guys—on the ice—is Bedard's happy place. He was the first skater on the ice that day for a 90-minute practice. Anders Sorensen, the head coach of the Blackhawks' AHL affiliate Rockford IceHogs, was in charge of getting the players ready for two games over the coming weekend.

Bedard wasn't joining a group of players he didn't know. Almost every player on the ice had taken part in the development camp in July after the draft—albeit without skates or sticks or pucks. That experience created a sincere camaraderie amongst the players in this camp, and it showed.

He also had a unique bond with four other players on the ice. In the days after Christmas, Bedard was the centerpiece of Canada's team at the World Junior Championship. That team, which won the gold medal, was loaded with current and future NHL draft picks, some of whom already had NHL experience.

Among the other talented players were defensemen Kevin Korchinski, Ethan Del Mastro, and Nolan Allan and forward Colton Dach—each of whom was a Blackhawks prospect already. When they received the championship trophy and skated around the ice absorbing the cheers from the fans, Bedard skated with Dach (whose arm was in a sling because of an injury suffered during the tournament) and Del Mastro, who was an assistant captain for Canada. He shared laughs with Korchinski. Their relationships now included a gold medal in an international tournament.

Fast forward to September. Bedard was joined on the ice by his four former World Juniors teammates, all of whom were on a text message chain that blew up when the Blackhawks

won the draft lottery in May. Korchinski, Allan, and Dach
were teammates with the Seattle Thunderbirds after the World
Juniors and had a game on the night of the draft lottery. That
game ended and each of them found celebratory texts from
Del Mastro waiting on their phones. There would be five
members of that great Canadian roster together in Chicago
soon.

Dennis Williams coached all five players for Canada at the
World Junior Championship—and against them as the head
coach of the Everett Silvertips in the WHL. He felt like a proud
parent watching the group skate together at professionals.

"It's great when you see them go through it together,"
Williams said. "I think it's a real feather in the cap for the
Chicago Blackhawks drafting such great players and great
teammates and great people. They're not only great hockey
players, but great ambassadors to the game and were great
teammates and were a big reason for our success at the World
Juniors."

Korchinski joined Bedard early on the ice for that first
practice of training camp in Chicago. They joked as they
skated, shot pucks on net, and got ready for what Sorensen
and his staff had waiting for them.

What became clear in that first practice was that Bedard was
different. Even with a collection of players who had enjoyed
individual successes in their junior and college careers, his
skill was evident. Bedard did things with the puck that others
couldn't imagine, much less execute. But he admitted there
was some rust to work off after spending time with the various
events required of a future NHL superstar. From taking pictures for hockey cards to talking to dozens of media members

in Las Vegas for a few days, Bedard hadn't been on the ice in what must have felt like forever for a self-described gym rat.

"Obviously, of course, there's been a lot of photos and interviews and everything, which is great," he said after skating in Chicago for the first time. "But I want to play hockey. That's what I love."

After a couple days of practice together in Chicago, the prospects flew to Minnesota for the two prospect games. For the first time in his career, Bedard would play in game action wearing a Blackhawks sweater.

The first game, which was streamed on YouTube for the fans who wanted to see Bedard's first "game" action, was played in a rink that usually houses rec league games. Not quite the 20,000-seat-capacity United Center, which would soon be filled with fans waiting to see Bedard start his regular season career on home ice.

It took Bedard more than one full period to make a mark on the scoresheet, and he didn't score Chicago's first goal in the game. Defenseman Louis Crevier, who stands almost a full foot taller than Bedard without skates on, was credited with breaking the St. Louis shutout bid.

But then Bedard went to work doing what he does best: scoring goals.

His first goal in a Blackhawks jersey came off a nice little drag move to find space. His release was already becoming legendary, and it was on full display on that shot. He ripped the shot through traffic and celebrated with a stick twirl that was reminiscent of golfer Chi Chi Rodriguez.

Bedard's second goal brought the wow factor. He danced through the defense to create space and unloaded a lethal shot from the goaltender's right that found a part of the net that others didn't see. Colton Dach, who was in front of the net creating traffic, raised his arms in both celebration and disbelief at the goal. Bedard acted like he had seen it before.

"I saw where it went," Bedard said after the game with a smile. "I saw a little far side, and it was kind of late on the power play, so I thought I'd go for it. Lucky it went in."

Luck had nothing to do with his third goal of the night, finishing a hat trick in a 5–0 Blackhawks win. Another shot that was behind the goaltender before he realized it was coming.

Fans who had questions about Bedard's ability to create against professionals were calmed, even if this game was against other prospects.

Fans who wanted highlights were thrilled.

And the Blackhawks' front office must have had smiles that could be seen from miles away.

"Looked alright," Sorensen joked after the game. "It's special, for sure. He looked dangerous every time he was on the ice."

The Blackhawks coaches, unofficially, had Bedard down for 11 shots on net. Three of them went in. Just another day at the office for the game's top prospect. It was another reminder of what was coming to the NHL in a few short weeks.

And Bedard was once again just happy to be "one of the guys."

"It doesn't mean too much, but it's nice to play games," Bedard said. "It was so much fun being with the guys, getting here, music is playing, and you just have that mojo going in. That was the best part, getting back into it. It was real competitive, so it's fun."

Blackhawks general manager Kyle Davidson was impressed with everything about Bedard in his first appearance on the ice in a Blackhawks sweater. The "elite" shot that has become Bedard's trademark was on display, and Davidson liked how much Bedard used it in game action. Like Bedard, he was quick to caveat that it was a prospect showcase against mostly other younger players, but the performance still popped.

Davidson was equally impressed with how well Bedard handled the busy schedule he kept going into and following the draft.

"It's been incredibly impressive," Davidson said of Bedard when he met with the media to kick off the new season. "The amount of attention, expectation—not just now but in the past—has been something that is rarely seen. I can't speak more highly of how he's handled it, how he's not let it impact his focus and what he thinks is important and the work he needs to put in, both on and off the ice, to perform at the level he expects of himself. Incredibly mature and impressive for an 18-year-old coming into a very unique situation."

Davidson spoke about the excitement in the organization and the fan base with Bedard's arrival. The unique situation Bedard was stepping into was the second full year of a rebuild under Davidson's guidance, but the shift in the trajectory of that rebuild rested largely on the shoulder of the 5'10" forward.

The Blackhawks announced their preseason training camp practices would once again be free and open to the public at Fifth Third Arena, the organization's practice rink, which sits a couple blocks away from the United Center. But the team was now requiring fans to secure tickets to watch the practices to make sure capacity at the practice arena, which is built more for youth league games than thousands of interested onlookers, could handle the crowds anticipated to watch the league's next superstar taking the ice with NHL players for the first time.

And those tickets sold out quickly, even with the first couple days happening during the work and school week at 10:00 AM. More than 250 fans reserved a spot at practices on Thursday, Friday, and Saturday mornings to be among the first to see Bedard in a Blackhawks jersey.

The first day of camp—Thursday, September 21—had a full house that arrived early and cheered when Bedard emerged from the dressing room. It wasn't a crazy ovation, but it was enough that it stood out. Never mind that the people in the stands could—should?—have been at work and/or school when he hit the ice.

Luke Richardson's first practice was working on and installing some defensive systems. There weren't a lot of *Did you see that?* moments from anyone, including Bedard. It was a hockey practice.

Following the skate, the Blackhawks did some off-ice work and then sent individual players to speak to the media. The previous year, it had been Jonathan Toews and Patrick Kane answering questions about the pending end of their respective careers in Chicago and if/when they would waive their no-trade clauses to leave the only team they had represented as professionals. This year, Bedard was back in front of the cameras speaking about the polar opposite: the beginning of his professional career.

After his first official skate with NHL players, Bedard flashed his smile and answered questions like he has so many times before. But the Chicago media got to see a little more of his personality this time around. Bedard joked about

FaceTiming with his mom while trying to cook for himself, and then admitted he doesn't do it very often but just wanted to say something different with the media. When asked about what he had learned about Chicago now that he had spent more time in his new home city, Bedard noted the "drivers are intense." The teenager was learning about how Chicagoans handle their business on the roads, which might actually be scarier for him than facing opponents who have height and weight (and age) advantages on the ice in his first season.

Richardson didn't want the coaches to be the ones who were helping Bedard adapt to the next level as much as the veteran leaders. After Bedard's first practice, Richardson talked about trying to acclimate his new superstar into the league with ease.

"I am treating him just like I would treat anybody else," Richardson said on the first day of training camp. "I think what we count on is the veterans in the room and the tightness that we started to build last year to continue. I think peer-to-peer help is much more effective in this league.

"The coach just needs to have good relations with everybody, but also have a good plan in place and a good environment for [players] all to feel like they can come to me if they need to talk to me. If that's a rookie or that's a 38-year-old veteran, either one, they should be able to feel the same and have confidence in that to come into the coach's room at any point in time. But [players should] also count on one another, and I think a special guy like Connor.... I think the smart veterans on our team will love to hear his perspective of the game. The game is always evolving and what does [Bedard] have new that's going to come here and help us."

Richardson's perspective during his rookie season as a head coach in the league was remarkably helpful and helped steady the ship during turbulent times. His second season as an NHL head coach came with a completely different collection of scenarios and circumstances. No longer was he anticipating a fire sale and answering questions about which players might not be on the roster.

When Richardson mentioned veterans learning about the game from the next special star in the league, that showed a level of emotional intelligence that isn't common in the game. Accepting and using information from every individual on the roster is what made his first season in Chicago a relative success; the Blackhawks played well enough that they almost cost the front office a chance to draft Bedard. The draft lottery saved the day.

The second season of Richardson's tenure in Chicago started as a transition from being bad to developing the next generation. And training camp opened with some veterans surrounding the Blackhawks' young players who would not only provide leadership and bring experience to the ice, but also a few guys who had something to prove. One of those players was Taylor Hall, a former No. 1 overall pick in his own right.

Hall brought an almost uniquely perfect résumé to the Blackhawks' effort to surround Bedard with players who could help him succeed. Hall was not only a former top pick, but he had previously skated with five other No. 1 overall picks: Jack Hughes (2019–20) and Nico Hischier (2017–18) in New Jersey and Connor McDavid (2015–16), Nail Yakupov (2012–13), and Ryan Nugent-Hopkins (2011–12) in Edmonton.

When Hall skated with Hischier during his rookie campaign in New Jersey, he had his best season in the NHL. Hall won the Hart Trophy with 93 points that season. After playing a complementary role on the regular season record-setting Boston Bruins during the 2022–23 season, Hall was traded to Chicago and came in with hopes of showing the league that he could still play a top-six role.

Unfortunately, Hall was held out of the first two days of training camp because of a lower-body issue. But when he first appeared on the ice on the third day of camp, he immediately slotted on Bedard's left side. And after just one practice, Hall already saw some similarities between Hischier and Bedard.

"Nico was kind of a blessing for me that year to have a young guy come in and play center and have that youthful speed and that transition game that Nico was really good at," Hall said after his first practice. "That was great for me. We worked well together; obviously we had had a really successful season, and so did our team. [This team in Chicago] kind of mirrors the expectations that that Jersey team had before the season. A lot of people had written us off, but we ended up making the playoffs and had a really good season. I'm not saying that we're going to do that here, but there is a real opportunity to springboard this quote-unquote rebuild with a really solid season and that season we had a lot of young guys come in and play well and play big roles and I think that put them in a good spot for their careers and we're hoping to do the same thing here."

Hall talked about the things he learned in the game as a top pick himself, but also what he'd experienced skating with the other five players who had been in a similar position to Bedard.

"Looking back, I've played with Jack Hughes, Nico, Nuge, Yakupov, McDavid, so I've had all these questions before.... It's a lot different than when I came in. That was 2010 and there was no Twitter or Instagram. You weren't getting highlights on your phone 10 minutes after they happened. You're still watching *SportsCenter* at night—you're still getting the stories like it used to be. I think the expectations and the hype is a little bit different for [Bedard]. It's important for him, when he leaves the rink, to get away from hockey, find something to do to take his mind off it. It's a long year, and you can't just think about hockey all the time—especially as you get later on in your career. You have to leave the game at the rink, that way when you come back to it, it feels more fresh in your brain. Those are all things I've learned as I've played. It's not just me he can rely on. Corey Perry, [Nick] Foligno, there are a lot of guys in the room who have played big games."

Hall was traded to Chicago with another player who brought a great deal of leadership and experience with him: Nick Foligno. Foligno was a pending free agent at the time but quickly signed a one-year deal with the Blackhawks to stay on a team that was clearly still in a building situation—and that surprised some onlookers. He could have found a role with a team that was closer to a championship, but the situation in Chicago appealed to him.

If the Blackhawks wanted to replace the leadership in the room that departed with Jonathan Toews, Foligno may have been one of the best players in the league to do that naturally. Foligno is one of the most respected veterans in the entire league; he had been a captain before and won both the King Clancy Memorial Trophy and the Mark Messier NHL

Leadership Award in 2016–17 while in Columbus—where he was a teammate of a 22-year-old Seth Jones.

Foligno was one of the first players in Chicago who reached out to Bedard and they instantly connected. When the NHL training camp opened, during the first warm-up laps of his professional career, Bedard was talking to and laughing with Foligno on the ice. Their relationship was growing on the ice after the 35-year-old had invested time in helping the 18-year-old feel more comfortable becoming a professional hockey player.

Bedard and Foligno exchanged text messages throughout the summer as they were both preparing for their first seasons in Chicago. And Bedard shared that he had been over to Foligno's house for meals to get to know him and his family better.

Their relationship reminded Foligno of the start of his NHL career, when veterans invested their time and energy into helping him become more comfortable.

"I remember going over to [Daniel Alfredsson's] house and his four kids, I think I had more in common with them than I did with Alfie at the time," Foligno said. "So, it was funny to kind of go back to that and remember the feelings that I had, and how much those guys helped me. I'm really excited about just having that opportunity to pay it forward in that way."

Now 16 years later, it was Foligno's kids who were excited about the top prospect in the NHL coming over for dinner. While Foligno had taken Bedard under his wing, the teenager also impressed the veteran with his approach to the game.

"He's a great kid," Foligno added. "I mean, that's first and foremost. He's well-raised and you can see he's handled the pressures of being in the spotlight now for a really young age and probably unfairly in some ways with the world we live in, but he's handled it with class and professionalism, even at a young age."

When the Blackhawks held an intra-squad scrimmage to start the first full week of training camp on September 25, the two fast friends almost connected for a beautiful goal. Foligno jumped on for Hall during the first half of the session and streaked to the goal. Bedard threw a gorgeous saucer pass across the offensive zone to a wide-open Foligno, who just missed connecting with what could have been an easy goal.

In the room after the scrimmage as Bedard finished talking to the collected media, Foligno walked behind the scrum and made a comment just loud enough to get Bedard's attention. Bedard tossed back that the media asked about his whiff on the open net and Foligno, without missing a beat, replied, "I was worried if I scored you might not make the team."

During that first scrimmage, Bedard spent most of his time on the ice with Hall and Ryan Donato, a veteran who had signed with Chicago as a free agent after spending the previous two years in Seattle. The speed on that line popped on each shift, but they weren't mistake-free. Luke Richardson mentioned that Bedard had a lapse on defense that he made up for with a goal on the same shift. In front of another capacity crowd (on a Monday morning), Bedard scored twice in the scrimmage and was close to two assists.

Bedard's self-assessment was one of the personality attributes that many scouts and analysts talked about leading up to the draft. When asked about the play Richardson mentioned, that element of his approach to the game showed—but with a sense of humor.

"That was a terrible play at the start there. I don't know what I was doing…. You make mistakes and sometimes things go your way. Obviously, you're still learning stuff and I didn't try to give it to the other team. But it was nice to make it up at the end of the shift."

When pressed if that was a play he maybe got away with in junior and was now learning he couldn't do against NHL players, Bedard laughed. "I don't think I could get away with that in pee-wee hockey," he said. "I tried to sauce it, missed it, it happens. Not a smart play. You're going to do that sometimes and yeah, you learn from it."

Learning from mistakes was something everyone was watching every time Bedard took the ice in training camp, whether it was for a drill or a scrimmage. And that was only going to intensify as preseason games began, with television cameras on his every move. The older players frequently were asked about—or simply brought up on their own—that Bedard has handled the attention and pressure so well leading up to the NHL.

"He's got so much pressure, like media and everything," 21-year-old Lukas Reichel said after the first scrimmage of camp. "He's handled it so good. [At] 18 it's so hard to do it, but he's really mature about it. That's the biggest thing I like about him."

The first time something didn't necessarily go Bedard's way during training camp was in the second intra-squad scrimmage, which had two smaller rosters for more shifts. The highlight of the two 25-minute periods was Bedard executing a jaw-dropping pass over a few would-be defenders' sticks to find Hall perfectly in stride across the neutral zone. But the final score of the scrimmage was 6–3 in favor of the other side.

After the scrimmage, Foligno half-joked that Bedard was not happy that he lost—a scrimmage, in practice, against his teammates. Foligno said he was pouting. Which got a chuckle from the media and Foligno.

Two days later, Bedard was finally ready to take his first morning skate as an NHL player. Yes, it was before a preseason game in Chicago against the St. Louis Blues. But the opportunity to skate against another team—at the United Center—seemed to be the first inkling that Bedard's dream was about to come true.

"As I was talking to my dad today, I was like, 'I get to play in the United Center tonight; that's pretty unreal,'" Bedard told the media after the morning skate. He was one of the Blackhawks' young players who could barely contain their excitement at the opportunity to skate against an opponent, even if they did their best to hide it.

But for Bedard, even a preseason game felt like the first significant, "real" professional moment in one of the most anticipated prospect journeys to the NHL in history.

"That's big, kind of see the fans and everything," he continued. "I haven't seen the lineup but guys who are trying to make the NHL and guys who have played in the NHL, so that's going to be a good challenge. Something good to get used to and build off."

As always, Bedard tried to remain composed behind his youthful appearance, but you could tell he was excited to play in a *game*. After all, hockey is what he loves to do. And now he was starting to do just that on the highest stage in the game.

Bedard was in the starting lineup for the Blackhawks in their first preseason game, and the crowd let him and the organization know the excitement was back in the building. There was a roar when his name was announced that blew away the other skaters on the ice. And the performance of "The Star-Spangled Banner" was loud as well, something Bedard said he noticed after the game.

It took Bedard little time to start getting everyone's attention on the ice. On his second shift against NHL competition, he danced through defenders and deked Jake Neighbours, an NHL regular in the Blues' lineup, to get a shot on net. He looked comfortable on the ice from the opening faceoff—which he won.

He was credited with an assist on the Blackhawks' first goal of the night and looked good throughout the game. But the score was tied at the end of regulation. Which meant Bedard's first NHL game required overtime.

Bedard was on the ice for most of the overtime period, noticeably avoiding eye contact with the bench a few times so he couldn't be changed out. And late in the overtime period, he made a gorgeous pass to a streaking Andreas Athanasiou for the game-winning goal.

The highlights were all there. The crowd was thrilled. Social media blew up. Bedard's arrival, albeit in a preseason game, was happening.

And his head coach was very happy with the performance.

"I liked all the little plays...but also his compete level," Luke Richardson said after the game. "Like, he finished his check in the neutral zone on a few guys a few times. Great reads on backchecks. He was just getting there at the right time to get a stick on a puck. I think, obviously, reverse psychology works for him. He knows where they're going to make the plays. And he can get there and defend them as well. And he doesn't just hang around the red line or blue line; he'll play a full 200-foot-game."

Bedard was somewhat surprisingly more critical of his performance. There were some concerns from outsiders about how a player of his age, experience, and size would hold up against NHL players—especially in the faceoff circle. Bedard won 10 of 16 draws in the game and skated more than 21 minutes, but saw areas where he could personally improve.

"I think I can be a lot better," Bedard said after his first NHL action. "I didn't think I personally played great. It's really good to get the win—obviously [it's] preseason. Nothing's better than winning. But I felt good in the systems, which is a good thing. In the D-zone I felt pretty comfortable. But I think I can do a lot better."

While he was critical of some elements of his game, he fully acknowledged that he wanted to play—and had, in fact, avoided eye contact during overtime. Most fans and media members were excited by the possibilities of Bedard skating in a 3-on-3 situation in overtime. He was too. When asked about staying on the ice, he said that's what he wants to do.

"Yeah, I like hockey," he said, which received a good laugh from the media members in the room after the game. "I want to be on the ice.… I played 3-on-3 probably five, six days a week with everyone back home. So it's probably the most fun in my life. Yeah, I didn't want to get off."

When he did leave the ice in that overtime, it was briefly. And the last time he left the ice was after the horn sounded and "Chelsea Dagger," the Blackhawks' goal song, played, signifying a victory.

A victory in which Bedard had played a leading role.

As much as Bedard was relaxed and calm talking about his personal performance in the game, his teammates and coaches were thrilled. Kevin Korchinski, the team's first-round pick the previous year who was fighting to be on the NHL roster as a teenager in his own right, said the bench was impressed with how disciplined Bedard was in the defensive zone and the systems. His commitment to both ends of the ice was noticed as much by his teammates as it was by the fans and media members in the building.

Winning didn't happen very frequently for the Blackhawks the year before Bedard arrived; that's how they were in a position to win the draft lottery and select him. But it shouldn't come as a surprise that Bedard was happy with the team outcome. In junior, on behalf of Canada at international tournaments and even during scrimmages and prospect showcase games, it was always about the team and the outcome for Bedard.

Inside the arena you couldn't avoid Bedard's name, number, and likeness. The Blackhawks' merchandise and marketing teams had been busy since the draft, designing custom pucks, sweatshirts, T-shirts, hats—just about anything you could imagine—with 98 BEDARD on them. And they were selling. While the jerseys coming into the building were still a collection of past and present players, there was still a noticeable number of Bedard sweaters in the seats. And the number of fans buying the newly available Bedard merch was obvious with the number of fans walking the concourses with bags.

Video of Bedard's "I like hockey" answer went viral overnight. Everyone from the Blackhawks and NBC Sports Chicago to *Spittin' Chiclets* to just about every hockey blog, every social media account, and the NHL itself had graphics or sound bites posted with it. Obvious Shirts, a local Chicago company, partnered with the Blackhawks and had shirts reading "I Like Hockey" on sale by the middle of the afternoon the day after he said it.

The buzz wasn't contained to the United Center; it was strong outside of the arena as well. The morning after the game, NBC Sports Chicago—the Blackhawks' local rights-holder—reported the game was the network's highest-rated Blackhawks preseason telecast in 10 years, with a peak rating of more than 71,000 Chicago-market homes.

Bedard's "I like hockey" comment made it all the way back to Regina, where his former coach smiled at the familiarity of the statement from the Pats' most famous alum.

"I really enjoyed watching Connor playing his first three-on-three overtime in the NHL," Pats head coach Brad Herauf said. "And even [the media], even when he is talking, not looking at the coach [so he could] stay on the ice longer. I mean, you guys asked in the scrum after the game, and his response is, 'I like hockey.' That's Connor; that's his swagger, that's his confidence in his own abilities. He's 18 years old and he's not coming off the ice. He wants to play three, four minutes. That's the exact same way he's been [in] junior and the way he's always been his whole life. He wants that responsibility on a team, and nobody works harder away from the rink to accept that responsibility."

Bedard's next step in the preseason was his first road game—in Detroit. It was his first taste of the historic rivalry between the Blackhawks and Red Wings, albeit not a regular season contest. He was excited to get the feel for the road life in the NHL, but this wasn't like most road trips during the season. The Blackhawks held their morning skate in Chicago at their practice rink and flew into Detroit the afternoon of the game.

This game didn't work out as well as his first on home ice. Bedard struggled in the faceoff circle (he won five of 13) and failed to register a point in 20:52 of ice time.

He did execute a gorgeous one-on-one play where he danced around Detroit defenseman Simon Edvinsson. The 6'4" opponent was the sixth overall pick in the 2021 NHL Draft and had appeared in nine NHL games the previous year with Detroit, but he was caught off guard by Bedard's swift puck movement. The shot didn't score, but the crowd was enamored with the skill displayed by the Blackhawks' top prospect.

Chicago lost the game 6–1, and it was as much of a struggle as the final score would indicate. Bedard was clearly frustrated with a few shot and pass attempts that didn't find their intended destination. The Blackhawks' roster for that game didn't have as many NHL regulars as his first appearance, and many of the forward lines hadn't spent much time together in training camp yet.

It was the first taste of NHL adversity for Bedard. A learning moment on his path to opening night in Pittsburgh.

"I was thrilled," he said sarcastically after the morning skate a couple days later. "No, I think we were all really mad after that one. It was bad. Just the pride we have playing for this team and this organization, it always hurts when you lose, and it's no different whether it's camp, preseason, whatever. That one stung for sure."

The good news for Bedard was the next preseason game was against the same opponent, but this time the Red Wings were coming to Chicago 48 hours after the ugly loss on their ice. And the best salve for a stinging loss?

"You win the next game, you feel better," he said. "Hopefully we can do that tonight."

The Detroit game in Chicago was a flipped script from the game in Detroit. Bedard struggled out of the gate, not winning a faceoff in the first period. But as the game progressed, he found his groove. He picked up assists on go-ahead goals by Connor Murphy and Corey Perry; Perry's stood up as the game-winner. Bedard then scored his first goal against NHL competition in the closing minute of regulation to put the game away.

One might think Bedard would be excited to finally get on the board in his third preseason game, but his facial expression on the ice was seemingly underwhelmed.

The goal was a power play goal into an empty net. No flash. No dancing defenders. Just an easy shot into an open cage. The fact that he had seemingly downplayed his first goal against NHL competition came up when Luke Richardson met with the media postgame. The head coach initially joked about it, but then made the point that Bedard needs to appreciate success when and where it comes.

"I don't know if he even counts those, but I count them," Richardson said after the game. "He's hard on himself, so we're going to have to lighten him up and make sure he enjoys these times. Because wins in the NHL are hard to come by—and once it starts for real, they're really hard to come by. We have to make sure we enjoy the night and have a little fun when you win a game."

With the win over Detroit, Bedard started his NHL preseason career with two multi-point games in his first three appearances. The betting odds on his season point total were starting to increase. And the buzz around the league was growing louder. Seemingly every guest who appeared on NHL Network on Sirius XM radio was asked for their point total prediction for Bedard; the range was anywhere between the high 50s and more than 100.

Indeed, the only player in Chicago anyone was talking about was Bedard as the preseason inched closer to its end.

Internationally, hockey media barely noticed Taylor Hall's three assists in the win over the Red Wings. Between Chicago's fourth and fifth preseason games, Hall again talked about skating with a player who, like him, has to try to live up to being a No. 1 overall pick as a rookie. Now, a couple weeks after he initially reported to camp, the two had spent more time together during training camp and on the ice during preseason games—and their rapport was clearly developing on and off the ice.

Within one week of the start of the 2023–24 regular season, and with both Bedard and Hall likely to skate in only one of Chicago's two remaining preseason games, the veteran noted that Bedard's professionalism was one element that stood out about the young forward's approach to the game.

"The thing with [Bedard] is he's already such a pro. He conducts himself like a 26-year-old around the rink. He may not know how to make his own meals yet, but he certainly knows how to warm up for practices and do workouts and all that stuff," Hall said. "I know that doesn't sound like much, but that's something you really learn as you become an NHLer is how to be a pro and he's already got that down.

"So, I think you're going to see, as the games get going in the regular season, you're going to see a lot of improvement, just even period to period."

Bedard's fourth preseason game gave him ample opportunity to learn. Chicago hosted the Minnesota Wild and both teams had lineups comprising mostly NHL regulars. The Blackhawks had three of what appeared to be their starting forward lines and six defensemen who all figured to be on the opening-night roster; the Wild's lineup was filled with NHL regulars. In net for Minnesota was Marc-André Fleury, a future Hall of Famer who Bedard admitted before the game he had watched a lot growing up.

In the game, Bedard had a few bright moments, but a lot of the night was frustrating. Minnesota blocked five of his shot attempts and tried to keep him outside. He improved in the faceoff circle, but finished the game with no points and only two shots on net.

A shootout was required to decide the winner, and Bedard was the first skater over the boards for Chicago. For nearly two decades, either Jonathan Toews or Patrick Kane was the first name called when the Blackhawks were in that situation. But now it was Bedard's show.

He slowly approached Fleury and tried a series of moves before fumbling the puck. As he failed to get a shot on net, Fleury reached out and tripped him. As Bedard lay on the ice, the great goaltender skated past him, tapping him on the shin with his stick as if to say, "Welcome to the show, kid."

After the game, Luke Richardson's comments about Bedard's game were slightly more philosophical. When asked about Bedard seeming to start looking more to pass midway through the game, the Blackhawks' head coach noted that he trusts Bedard's instincts, but they might be able to show him some things on film to help him.

"We're always going to want more out of our players," Richardson said. "We'd like them to shoot the puck more…. But he's the one who sees it on the ice, [and] he sees it different than us. So we're going to have to trust a guy with that kind of talent and vision, when he thinks it's right to shoot or when he thinks it's right to hold onto the puck or make a play."

Bedard didn't skate in the Blackhawks' final preseason game, instead staying home with a number of veterans the organization wanted to keep healthy for the coming days. The real test would come when the games mattered. The regular season was right around the corner, and Connor's childhood hero, Sidney Crosby, was waiting for him on opening night.

Bedard finished the preseason with one goal and four assists in four preseason games. He led the Blackhawks with 16 shots on net. While his numbers on a larger level seemed good, it seemed like Bedard wasn't happy with his overall performance during his four appearances.

He displayed the pause and thoughtfulness he's become known for with each media scrum, though. While he might not have been happy with the lack of goals, he also made it clear that he understood the learning curve of an 18-year-old NHL rookie, and while he was coming into the league with all of the hype and expectations of any prospect in recent memory, those would still happen for even him.

On Monday, October 9, the Blackhawks announced their official opening-night roster for the 2023–24 season. Bedard's name was on there, meaning the end of him working hard just to make the team and a transition to making an impact in the league.

The Blackhawks' practice rink was filled to capacity; it was a holiday in Chicago, so school was off all over the city. The stands were packed with kids who shouted Bedard's name throughout the hour-long practice before the team collected their gear and took off for the airport. Their flight—Bedard's first as an NHL player—would be that afternoon. The work was about to begin.

"I'm so excited," Bedard said after practice. "It's hard to think about and realize it's true, but it's really exciting. You don't know what to expect, but over the summer I feel like I've worked as hard as I possibly could to prepare myself. I think for me it's just letting instincts take over and really enjoying it."

"I'm sure I will [have butterflies]. It's a big moment. In the end I think for me it's taking the anthem and obviously their player announcement and the warm-up and have that be the 'oh my God' moment and then once the game starts I want to be focused on the game and not be starstruck as much. But I think that first bit's going to be pretty crazy."

How was business for the Blackhawks as the season drew near? The Blackhawks had nearly doubled their full and partial season ticket packages for the 2023–24 season. Overall, the Blackhawks were expecting a 17 percent increase in ticket sales and 26 percent bump in revenue over their projections for Bedard's rookie campaign.

According to the organization, in the first three months into the fiscal year for the 2023–24 season, the Blackhawks already nearly doubled their total merchandise sales compared with the same time frame for the previous year (first three months into the 2022–23 season). The organization didn't know yet at the start of the regular season where Bedard's jersey sales would rank across the entire league, but among the thousands of No. 98 jerseys sold since they officially went on sale on June 28, approximately 85 percent of those sold were authentic jerseys. And those impressive numbers were only through the team's directly linked channels (web, on-site store, and Michigan Avenue location).

Before the first game of the regular season, the NHL announced that since the draft concluded and it became available, Bedard's jersey was the No. 1 seller in the league online in the U.S. and Canada—ahead of established NHL veterans Jack Hughes, Brad Marchand, Sidney Crosby, and David Pastrňák.

Bedard was driving offense on the ice and dollars at the box office. He was also selling jerseys, T-shirts, hats, coffee mugs, personalized pucks. Whatever aspect of the Blackhawks organization you can think of, Bedard was improving it by being on the roster.

Now, the hard part began. It was off to Pittsburgh for Game 1 of Connor Bedard's NHL career.

CHAPTER 3

THE BEGINNING

He's one of the most ready players I've ever seen come in at 18.
—TAYLOR HALL

O N OCTOBER 5, 2005, Sidney Crosby made his NHL debut. One of the most highly regarded prospects in recent memory at that time—before social media—was the No. 1 overall player selected in the 2005 NHL Draft and headed straight to the league.

Crosby skated 15:50 in the game and picked up his first career point—an assist on a Mark Recchi power-play goal at 5:36 into the third period. That was the only goal Pittsburgh would score that night in a 5–1 loss to the New Jersey Devils.

Connor Bedard was 80 *days* old.

Obviously Bedard doesn't remember that game for Crosby, but he will undoubtedly remember the night of October 10, 2023, for the rest of his life. In the 18 years and five days since making his debut, Crosby had established himself as one of the greatest players in the history of the NHL and an icon in Canada—three Stanley Cup championships, a golden goal for Canada at the 2010 Winter Olympics, eight All-Star Game appearances, two Hart Trophies, two Conn Smythe Trophies, the 2010 Mark Messier Leadership Award, and being named to the NHL's 100th anniversary team in 2017.

Like thousands of other young hockey players, Crosby was a hero for Bedard. Chicago's new rookie spoke frequently, from the day the schedule was released until the day before his own debut, about facing the future Hall of Famer. The nerves would be there; he knew they would be. But once the puck dropped, Bedard's hope was that he could focus on the game itself.

Was he nervous? One of the first questions Bedard was asked when he met with a crowd of media in Pittsburgh was simple: How did he sleep the night before his NHL debut? "Like a baby."

"I don't want to start the game being starstruck or anything," Bedard continued. "I kinda want the warm-up and anthem and everything to be that moment for me and then once the game starts—like the games I played in the past—I want to be the best version of myself, and we want to win the game. Take it shift by shift and see how it goes."

When asked what a younger Connor would think of him making his debut against Crosby, of all players, he chuckled. "Six-year-old Connor would be pretty fired up."

The cameras were predictably everywhere Bedard went in Pittsburgh. He had a media scrum before the game that looked like it was a playoff game or, for him, the World Juniors. There were more bodies than the room could hold.

That was one element of Bedard's arrival in the league that didn't get talked about as much. The amount of time he had spent in front of cameras from the time he started to generate buzz in western Canada as a younger teenager had prepared him for this moment. His junior coaches and coaches with Hockey Canada had talked about how it felt like the Beatles—or perhaps now, Taylor Swift—were at the arena for a lot of his final two junior seasons because of the buzz around his game.

When the lights turned on and the mics closed in, he didn't flinch. Many other rookies can get caught off guard, even those who had won medals for Canada in the World Juniors. Some found their way to the *ums* and *ahs* frequently as they tried to find the right words to say to the collection of reporters staring at them. Not Bedard. The 18-year-old stood in front of them, composed and smiling, answering questions for nearly 10 minutes.

Hours later, when it was time for the Blackhawks to get off their team bus—again, in front of a horde of cameras, because this game was kicking off the league's entire season on ESPN—there was Bedard, front and center. He arrived at the rink in a nicely tailored pinstripe suit that got the fashion treatment from ESPN's P.K. Subban after the game. Fully approved by the network's expert in dress before games.

Taylor Hall remembered being a top overall pick and the struggles he had on a bad Edmonton team trying to find his way on the ice against NHL players. Young players often come into the league and defer too much. But Hall was confident that Bedard's maturity would show when he was skating against the world's best players.

"He knows the strengths of his game when he plays to them," Hall said. "Where a lot of young guys come in and they don't maybe know how they need to play, where really you just want to be the best version of yourself. And I think Connor knows that. I think he knows exactly what kind of player he is and what he wants to be. And you can tell he watches a lot of hockey. He loves the game."

The cameras searching for anything and everything Bedard-related created some unlikely buzz just before the game when he and Kevin Korchinski were going to lead the team onto the ice. It appeared Bedard's stick had moved from where he left it.

Bedard's routine was to have his stick waiting, with the blade off the ground, by itself on the way to the ice. It wasn't where he left it, so he had to run back in the room and grab another. And, of course, there were cameras there to catch it. Social media lit up with a flurry of posts along the lines of "Bedard's so nervous he forgot his stick." In reality, veterans had simply pranked Bedard, treating him like any other rookie.

Bedard (18 years old) and Korchinski (19) were two of the six Blackhawks making their first appearance in an NHL opening-night game. And they were the youngest players in the NHL at their respective positions. The rookies were given their "welcome to the NHL" lap before the rest of the team joined them on the ice. And the two took their lap in style; neither had a helmet on—but they both had a smile you could see all the way back in Chicago.

As is the tradition, the players making their debut knock the pucks on the ice, take their first shot, and skate a lap before their teammates join them. Finally, we saw some nerves from Bedard. He whiffed on his shot attempt before the veterans took the ice.

Whenever he was asked about being nervous for his first game, Bedard said he hoped to get the emotions out of his system during warm-ups and the anthem. When he was shown on television during the anthem, you could sense he was excited. When his name was announced in the starting lineup, the Penguins' home fans booed him. Because, at the end of the day, Bedard might be one of the most exciting players to come into the league in years, but he was still the wrong team's star player.

Then it was time for the moment he had dreamt about his entire life. And the opening faceoff of his NHL career would be against Sidney Crosby—his hero.

The NHL had veteran official Kelly Sutherland working the game, and he had a mic on for the event. After making a brief comment to Crosby, he turned to the young man in the white No. 98 sweater and said, "Connor. Welcome to the NHL, man." Bedard said, "Thank you," and the puck dropped.

Crosby won the faceoff. Because of course he did.

The expectations for Bedard were high on the ice. Every shift he took was hyper-focused during the broadcast. If he got hit, the hockey world held its collective breath to see how quickly he would get up. When would he unleash his first rocket of a shot in the NHL? Would he score a goal in his first game? How many perfect storylines would follow the initial faceoff against Crosby?

The responsibilities Bedard had to shoulder in his first NHL game around the game were significant as well. After facing a postseason-level media group before the game, he then needed to get in front of more cameras during the game. During the first intermission he spoke with ESPN. During the second intermission he was featured in an interview on Sportsnet in Canada.

Everyone wanted a piece of Bedard.

"It's serious stuff," Blackhawks GM Kyle Davidson said when he met with the media in Pittsburgh before the game.

"The attention, the level of demand on him has been very high, unlike anything that I've seen for a young player since I've been around the Blackhawks. He's handled it with a maturity so far beyond 18 years. It's been really impressive to watch.

"He's handled it very well and I have no hesitation he's going to continue to handle it in a very professional manner."

During the second period, with the Blackhawks trailing 2–0, Bedard made a subtle pass to defenseman Alex Vlasic—who was one of the other Blackhawks skaters in his first career opening night—who set up veteran forward Ryan Donato for the Blackhawks' first goal of the season.

With a secondary assist on the play, Bedard notched his first career NHL point.

He became the youngest player to register a point in his NHL debut in 10 years and the second-youngest player to have a point in franchise history, behind only Eddie Olczyk. And, according to the NHL, he did it roughly 10 minutes faster than Crosby registered his first point—also an assist—in his debut. When, again, Bedard was just 80 days old.

The Blackhawks came into the game with long odds of winning. The Penguins had made a number of veteran additions to their roster, including reigning Norris Trophy winner Erik Karlsson, and were very public about their desire to get back to being a championship-caliber team. So when the score was 2–0, it felt like the young Blackhawks were in for a long night.

But that first goal, which started with Bedard, initiated a comeback. Chicago scored four unanswered goals and skated away with a seemingly improbable win.

Bedard skated a heavy workload that night. His 21:29 led all Blackhawks forwards and was three minutes more than Crosby on the other side. While he struggled in the faceoff circle—Bedard won just two of 13 draws—he led the Blackhawks in shots on goal (five) and shot attempts (11). He did what he had always done—Connor Bedard drove offense for his team.

And he drove eyeballs to ESPN. The day after the game, Disney—ESPN's parent company—reported Bedard's NHL debut averaged 1.43 million viewers, making it the most-watched regular season NHL game ever on cable (excluding the Winter Classic). Viewership was up an eye-popping 92 percent over the similar opening-night window the previous year, which had featured the Tampa Bay Lightning and New York Rangers.

As we saw in previous big moments in his hockey life, Bedard's comments after his first NHL game were as focused on the team and his teammates as they were on his own personal performance, even if the questions he fielded were largely about his experience.

"It was a lot of fun," he said after the game. "To get the win, obviously being down two and coming back like we did was awesome for our group. I think you remember it with a little better taste in your mouth when you win. So, it was awesome for me and Kev [Korchinski] to have that experience."

The celebration surrounding his first game and first point was short-lived. The team left PPG Paints Arena in Pittsburgh and went straight to the airport; Chicago had a game the next night in Boston against Bedard's first Original Six opponent.

Television coverage on ESPN of Bedard's first NHL game overwhelmed the fact that Crosby and the Penguins were celebrating their home opener. With TNT handling his second career game—and the Blackhawks' first nationally televised game of the year—that wouldn't be as easy. The Bruins were beginning their centennial season and celebrated their

100th anniversary with a parade of all-time greats before the start of the game.

The pregame ceremony included family members of Bruins legends who had passed and many of the greats from past championship games. Bedard was asked if he wanted some retribution for the Bruins' 2011 championship with some of those players in the building; Boston had defeated his favorite team, the Vancouver Canucks, to win the Stanley Cup that year. He said it wasn't a factor but joked that he was a "pretty upset six-year-old" when the Bruins raised the Cup in Vancouver.

As they introduced the players whose numbers have been retired by the franchise, in walked Phil Esposito and Bobby Orr. With all those legends in the building, Bedard waited little time to check another box on his list of career firsts.

At 5:37 into the first period, Bedard found a loose puck behind the net, grabbed it, and put a wrap-around shot into the net for his first career NHL goal.

The excitement on the ice from his teammates was visible joy. Taylor Hall had an enormous smile on his face as he approached the rookie for a group hug. As Bedard approached the bench, Nick Foligno looked like the proudest father in the arena—even if Bedard's own dad was in the stands with his heart beating through his shirt.

"It was exciting," Bedard said after the game. "It's a big relief, too. You wanna get one really bad, quick to get it out of the way. It was a cool moment and a cool building to do it in…. It's a moment so many people in the world dream of. I'm very fortunate to be able to be put in this position and get a chance like that."

The goal impressed his coach, too.

"He just knows where to go," Luke Richardson said postgame. "He's one of those guys that has instincts and he picked up that rebound and knew that he had time and room, but he did it pretty quick. It was really fun to watch."

As the game progressed, Bedard experienced the first adversity of his NHL career. Hall was hit from behind on the first shift of the second period and left the ice favoring his left arm. He returned for one brief shift on a power play later in the period but was shut down for the rest of the night.

The Blackhawks coaches had to put their lines in a blender to come up with combinations that might work as they struggled to generate offense against a good, veteran Bruins team. In the third period, Bedard received a pass from Lukas Reichel and attacked the net. As he shot the puck, he got tripped and crashed into the boards hard. He stayed down for a moment in discomfort, and the hearts of Blackhawks fans—of hockey fans everywhere—skipped a beat.

But Bedard got back up and stayed on the ice for another shift.

Chicago lost the game 3–1. The photo of Bedard with the puck from his first assist showed his enormous smile; the photo of him with the puck from his first goal was more somber. You could tell the outcomes of the two games just looking at the two images.

Any question about his body after the big collision in the third period was dismissed quickly after the game. "Yeah, I'm great." And he moved on to the next question in another crowded postgame dressing room.

The executives at Turner would agree with that statement. Yes, Bedard was great—for ratings. Again. After the phenomenal audience ESPN had drawn for the season's opening night, the eyeballs returned the following night to watch Bedard again on TNT. The Blackhawks–Bruins game averaged 917,000 total viewers on TNT, making it the network's second-largest recorded viewership of a regular season game behind the 2022 Winter Classic (which is the only regular season game on a cable network to outdraw Bedard's debut on ESPN).

Two games into Bedard's NHL career, he was catching eyeballs all over North America. It's worth noting that Major League Baseball had playoff games airing against both of Bedard's first two games.

After two games in two days against teams with championship-pedigree players across their lineups, the Blackhawks got a break for a couple days before playing their third game as the road team in a home opener. The third game of the year would present another unique moment for Bedard. He headed back to Canada for the first time, playing in Montreal against the Canadiens. Another Original Six matchup, but this game would have additional significance because it was his first in his home country.

It was also the first time Bedard would be featured on *Hockey Night in Canada*.

"I can't wait," he said when speaking with the studio crew on Sportsnet from the ice during warm-ups. "Obviously growing up I always got excited for Saturday nights. It's pretty cool to be a part of it and a cool building and a special place to play, so we're all pretty excited."

The media crowd waiting for him in the dressing room in Montreal was bigger than what he'd seen in Boston, close to what he had for his first game in Pittsburgh. He was the focus of the pregame media in both the U.S. and Canada; this was also his first game on Chicago's television rightsholder,

NBC Sports Chicago. Even though he hadn't officially been an NHL player for a full week, Bedard was establishing himself as a nightly must-watch. And the Blackhawks' media relations team was inundated daily with requests to speak with him.

Montreal opened its barn with a raucous crowd and the Blackhawks did not have a good start. Without Taylor Hall in the lineup, the Blackhawks offense struggled until scoring twice in the third period to make the game interesting before ultimately losing 3–2. Chicago was 0-for-7 on the power play, which didn't sit well with Bedard or fans on social media. Bedard was credited with one assist in the game, making him one of the 10 youngest players in NHL history to record a point in his first three games. The league and media outlets in Chicago as well as across Canada and the United States were starting to pay close attention to the number of short-lists for which Bedard was qualifying as the youngest player in the NHL.

After the game Bedard was once again solemn—remember, he hates losing. For his first game as an NHL player in one of the biggest markets in the league, Bedard heard frequent in-game boos for the first time in his career. "Yeah, I love it," he said when asked about hearing the boo birds. It's a badge of honor for a road player to get that treatment every single time he touches the puck for three full periods, especially when it's his first game and there isn't bad blood from a previous game.

Connor's parents, Tom and Melanie, were in the building in Montreal to watch his Canadian debut. His mother joked after the game about the boos but remained impressed with how he had adapted to the NHL life early in his career.

"Connor just really loves the game," Melanie Bedard told Dave Stubbs of NHL.com after the loss to the Canadiens. "I don't think that to this point he's paid too much attention to the pressure, he's just a regular guy who loves hockey.

"It sounds cliche, but he's been so fortunate on the whole journey to have had amazing teammates and coaches. Tom and I are both impressed and sometimes a little surprised by how he does handle himself in all of this."

There was a strong group of media waiting for Bedard—again—when the Blackhawks arrived in Toronto for their off-day practice on that Sunday. Taylor Hall, who was recovering from the shoulder injury he suffered in Boston, said after the practice that he had some concerns about Bedard seemingly doing in-game and pregame interviews every night. Not necessarily in a bad way, but the amount of attention on Bedard was standing out to a veteran teammate who, like Bedard, had once been the top overall pick.

The attention didn't appear to get under Connor's skin, however. He understood the season-opening trip and the locations of the games were going to increase the want/need for him to talk to the media. After all, he was surrounded by media and fans during his final junior season and, especially, during his historic performance leading Canada to gold during the last two World Junior Championships.

Something that did get Bedard's attention, and put a big smile on his face, was a surprise at practice on that Sunday in Toronto. Representatives from Hockey Canada arrived with boxes for both Bedard and Kevin Korchinski—their championship rings from the 2023 World Junior Championship. The two rookies showed off their beautiful hardware to veterans Nick Foligno and Corey Perry.

Whoever made the NHL schedule for the 2023–24 season built in some storylines early for the Blackhawks. In Montreal,

Bedard played against Juraj Slafkovsky, the No. 1 overall pick in 2022. Two nights later, he would be in Toronto to skate against one of the players Bedard talked about a lot during his development: Auston Matthews.

Matthews, like Bedard, Crosby, and Slafkovsky, was also a No. 1 overall pick. As was one of Matthews' teammates, John Tavares. Before the end of November, Bedard and the Blackhawks would face 12 of the 18 previous No. 1 overall picks in the NHL draft leading up to Bedard's selection in 2023. And three of the other six—Taylor Hall (a teammate), Patrick Kane (still an unsigned free agent while returning from injury) and Nail Yakupov (no longer in the NHL)—weren't options for Bedard to skate against.

But facing Matthews was going to be special. He's known for his shot, like Bedard. One of the elite scorers in the game, Matthews made history of his own early in the season; he recorded a hat trick in both of the Leafs' first two games.

After their respective Sunday off-day practices, Matthews said Bedard's shot is as good as anyone he's ever seen. Bedard was asked about that comment and skating against a player he admittedly followed in the league.

"He's someone that I feel kind of pioneered a certain shot and he's got 6 and 2, so he's doing something right. Ever since he came into the league, he's been someone I've loved to watch and looked up to just how he plays the game. His shot is obviously something everyone knows about but just his complete game, how he is in his own end and how he is all around the ice, is pretty special. Because he scores so many goals and is so good in the offensive zone, I think that gets overlooked. I'm excited to go up against him."

One of the minor storylines—well behind the matchup with Matthews—heading into the game in Toronto was Bedard's friendship with a rookie in the other room: Maple Leafs center Fraser Minten. Minten was a second-round pick by the Leafs in the 2022 NHL Draft and made their team out of camp. During the 2018–19 and 2019–20 seasons, Minten and Bedard were teammates in bantam at West Van Academy and became good friends. Bedard lived with Minten in Toronto when they were both working out there during the summer before their respective rookie years and exchanged excited text messages when they both made the opening-night rosters for their teams.

When the puck dropped in Toronto, the arena was once again excited for a game that was being nationally televised on a Monday night. The Leafs were considered a contender to win the Stanley Cup and having an Original Six team in the barn always brought out the most from the fans in the NHL's largest Canadian market.

After a less-than-stellar effort in Montreal, the Blackhawks came out more physical in the first period. The game was tied at zero after 20 minutes, but Chicago's defense was playing well. For his part, Bedard's line was dominant against Matthews' line, even if Connor hadn't won a faceoff.

We saw some visible frustration from Bedard during this game that we hadn't seen before. At one point he ripped a shot on net but missed, and dropped his head in disgust. As he skated to the bench, Bedard smashed his stick against the boards.

When the final horn sounded after a wild end of the third period that saw two video reviews overturn goals— one for each team—inside the final minute of regulation, the

Blackhawks departed with a 4–1 win. It was the second win on the Blackhawks' gauntlet road trip to open the season, and the best effort from the team as a whole.

But Bedard finished without a point for the first time in his NHL career. He spent most of the night skating directly against Matthews' line with Mitch Marner and Tyler Bertuzzi; Bedard was on the ice for 8:40 against Matthews directly. Bedard's line had 13 shot attempts to Matthews' lines' seven.

The Montreal and Toronto games were exciting, Original Six matchups—and the first two games featuring Bedard on NBC Sports Chicago. After huge ratings on nationally televised games to start his career, how did the local rightsholder broadcasts perform? Bedard's first two appearances on the network averaged a 2.0 rating—a 233 percent increase compared with their telecasts of the Blackhawks' first two regular season games the previous year. The network also reported a peak of over 112,000 Chicago market homes tuning in to the game against the Maple Leafs.

Bedard was driving eyeballs everywhere.

With one game left on the road trip to start his career, the next test would include another former No. 1 overall pick on a team the Blackhawks coaches and front office were using as the model of their rebuild: the Colorado Avalanche.

Like Matthews, Nathan MacKinnon was an elite offensive player. Like Matthews, MacKinnon won the Calder Trophy as the league's rookie of the year after he was the No. 1 overall pick in the draft. But unlike Matthews, MacKinnon has a Stanley Cup championship ring.

When the Blackhawks hired Luke Richardson as their head coach, general manager Kyle Davidson and Richardson both talked about one of their "interviews" taking place at a bar in Chicago watching the Avalanche and Tampa Bay Lightning in the 2022 Stanley Cup Final. The consensus was that those two teams were the models the Blackhawks needed to emulate if they wanted to compete at a championship level in the future.

This game stacked up as an early test for the young Blackhawks against a team the coaches and front office wanted them to look and play like into the future. And, once again, it would air nationally in the United States on ESPN.

It was also the final game on a five-game, 10-day road trip, and the fourth time in five games the Blackhawks would play the role of visitor in a home opener. And, after the team had flown almost 3,000 miles, the game was played at altitude in Denver.

A perfect storm was waiting for the Hawks, and the final box score looked and felt like a team that had simply run out of gas. After playing even hockey for the first nine minutes of the first period, the Avalanche skated the Blackhawks out of the building. The 4–0 final score may not have been a huge surprise to many, but Bedard being held without a shot attempt in the game was the first statistical outlier of his young career.

"[Playing in home openers has] been a lot," he said. "For me, coming into the league and getting those moments—crowds are always great but, especially on the first night, everyone's excited and the building's pretty energized. So that was really cool for me and a lot of the younger guys, I'm sure. But it's good you don't have to wait as long to start the game."

The Blackhawks landed back in Chicago around 3:00 AM Central Time the next day. Richardson gave the team a day off to get some rest, but they only got the one day—the defending Stanley Cup champion Vegas Golden Knights were coming to Chicago for the Blackhawks' home opener on Saturday night.

Chicago knows how to throw a party, and the Blackhawks' home opener was certainly a reminder of that. Hundreds of fans lined up on Madison outside the United Center along a red carpet four hours before puck drop to cheer for the players as they were individually introduced. A DJ played, a drumline performed, and the fans cheered, all on a windy, overcast afternoon that saw the temperature outside the arena drop about 20 degrees between that day's morning skate and the pregame festivities.

Once the players navigated the fans begging for autographs, they attempted to settle in for some amount of business as usual. But for a few young players in the room—including Bedard—this would be their first time skating in a home opener at the United Center. Even though the Blackhawks were under .500 coming home from the trip, there wasn't an empty seat by the time the official ceremonies began. With rally towels that included red LED lights, the larger lights went down in the house as the players skated out to ovations.

When Connor Bedard emerged through the lights and smoke at the end of the rink, the ovation was thunderous.

Following the introductions of the players, the organization shared an emotional tribute to Rocky Wirtz. Many fans cried when they showed a folding chair behind Section 119—where Rocky had sat for so many years—with his name sewn into the back and yellow roses.

After that incredible moment, Jim Cornelison stepped to his usual place on the red carpet on the ice just in front of the penalty boxes to perform "The Star-Spangled Banner." Even players who had been with the Blackhawks for a few years, like Connor Murphy and Seth Jones, hadn't heard a packed house cheer through the anthem with that level of vigor; it felt like a playoff atmosphere for the first time in years.

If the Blackhawks wanted to see a rebirth with their fan base in the stands, this was it.

Then the puck dropped and the game started. Like every other game.

But this wasn't like the first five games of Bedard's career to that point. It was at home, and there were even more cell phone flashes going off when he took the ice to warm up. You could see the flashes go off as seemingly everyone in the arena took a photo of the opening faceoff—which he won.

It didn't take long for the action to elevate the excitement in the building. The Blackhawks got a power play just 85 seconds into the contest, and Bedard stayed on the ice. Chicago lost the faceoff to start the power play, but Taylor Hall dug the puck out of the corner and found Bedard all alone about 15 feet in front of the net.

Bedard ripped his patented shot and it found pay dirt. His first shot at the United Center in a game that mattered went in.

And the roof just about blew off the United Center.

The place was up for grabs as the players congratulated Bedard. For many fans, the moment celebrating Rocky Wirtz before the game felt like a transition moment. Bedard scoring on his first shot felt like an exclamation point. And when we learned that the last Blackhawks rookie to score on his first shot at the United Center was Jonathan Toews, the passing of the torch felt more than just symbolic.

Unfortunately for Bedard, his teammates, and the nearly 20,000 fans in the arena that night, Vegas remained undefeated.

And it was a defensive miscue by Bedard and Seth Jones that allowed Vegas to break a 2–2 tie just seconds into the third period.

After the game, Bedard was asked about scoring his first goal on home ice. As he had been after previous losses, he was able to acknowledge that he would be able to reflect on the special moment at some point. But he was focused on his perceived error in defensive coverage that led to the go-ahead goal.

"That third goal was definitely my fault," he said. "Can't start a period like that. That's something I've got to be better in, and I know that and everyone knows that."

Coming "home" to Chicago for his fifth home opener was yet another unique experience early in Bedard's career. There were plenty of cameras at the morning skate and waiting for him after the game. The first two weeks of the regular season were a grind against good teams, leaving the team—and Bedard—little time to catch their breath and take stock of their performances.

The volume of cameras and microphones waiting for Bedard constantly continued to get attention, even now that he was at the United Center. After an emotional home opener, Bedard acknowledged that the ceremonies that had proceeded five of the six games he had played in and the number of cameras that had been around him were in fact starting to be a lot. Some amount of "normal" as the regular season continued couldn't come quickly enough.

"[The media attention] has been pretty wild," Bedard said. "Ever since before camp-ish, it's been crazy, but it's not something I look at as a negative at all. I'm really grateful to be in the position I am and there's very few people that get that opportunity, get to be as lucky. I'm looking at it like that.

"I'm living out a dream and I feel very fortunate for that. But it is crazy and busy. I'm human too; I can get a little tired. But it's been good and I'm just enjoying it."

CHAPTER 4

GAME-BREAKER

WITH THE BLACKHAWKS' SERIES of home openers in the rearview mirror, there was some hope that the team—and Bedard—could find some level of regularity in their hockey lives. Unfortunately, the schedule wasn't doing them any favors. Chicago's second home game would feature their second game against the Boston Bruins in less than two weeks.

Boston came into the game undefeated with a chance to set the best mark to start a season in the 100-year history of the franchise. The Blackhawks, on the other hand, put Taylor Hall on injured reserve because of a shoulder injury and activated Philipp Kurashev for the first time in the regular season. So, more lineup changes and a strong team on the other side.

The game was being played on a wild night across the NHL. All 32 teams were in action for just the second time in league history, and ESPN had billed the night the "Frozen Frenzy." The league and network had marketed the night for weeks leading up to the slate of games, with Boston–Chicago being one of the marquee matchups—which meant more cameras and interviews for the Blackhawks.

But not as much for Bedard this time. He didn't talk to the media after the morning skate, and the focus of the broadcast was centered more on the games around the league than solely on Bedard's play. That didn't mean the announcers forgot he was on the roster, though; he was still a focal point of their commentary. And a near-sellout crowd of 19,370 was excited for the Original Six matchup early in the season.

Early in the first period the Blackhawks got a power play. Like Vegas had done in Chicago's home opener, Boston somehow left Bedard all alone in front of the net and he rifled home what appeared to be the first goal of the night. After the puck hit the back of the net, Bedard dropped to a knee and appeared to use Patrick Kane's "Heartbreaker" celebration. The United Center was, once again, up for grabs. Between the goal and the celebration, the house was rocking.

Until the official announced Boston was challenging the play, which it believed was offside.

After a lengthy review, the goal was indeed taken off the board. Bedard appeared dejected on the bench, as were his teammates. The energy in the building deflated as well.

The Blackhawks played tough for two periods but once again found small mistakes cost them in big ways. For the second time in three games, Chicago was shut out (by an undefeated team). Bedard's goal coming off the board also meant he had been held without a shot on net for the second time in the three-game span. After putting a record number of shots on net in the Blackhawks' first four games, he was held to just two shots on net total by Colorado, Vegas, and Boston.

The veterans in the room weren't worried about Bedard or any of the other young Blackhawks getting frustrated, even if they were upset with their personal performances.

"The young energy is great," veteran defenseman Jarred Tinordi said after the game. "You don't want them to be too calm out there. They're good players and they're here for a reason. There's a reason those guys are in this room. They can handle these moments; they can handle playing the minutes that they're playing. We saw it in training camp; we've seen it here at the start of the year."

Even with the national television network in the building, Bedard didn't talk after the game. Tinordi, Corey Perry, and Philipp Kurashev were in the room to answer tough questions about another loss.

After the game, head coach Luke Richardson spoke about having time to work on the little things that had plagued the Blackhawks in the early season. And the Blackhawks would have plenty of time to catch their breath and work on things as their schedule slowed down dramatically. Chicago was one of the first teams in the league to play seven games. Following the Bruins game, the Blackhawks would play only two games in the next 10 days and six in the next 22.

The competition wasn't going to get any easier, though. The Blackhawks had a trip to Vegas and games against the defending Eastern Conference champion Florida Panthers, the New Jersey Devils, and the Tampa Bay Lightning coming up. But they would have some time to get healthy and reinforce their systems in practices. When asked about the Blackhawks' strength of schedule early in the season, Bedard liked the challenge.

"Obviously they're great teams, but it's the NHL; every team is really good," he said the day before the game in Vegas. "We've got to learn how to get to that level and beat these top teams. It's really good for us to have that [compete level] in these games we're playing here. Cup champs two of three, and Boston and Colorado, that's great. That's good for us to go against them, but we've obviously got to start winning here."

The coaches weren't happy about the performance against Boston, so after an off day the Blackhawks had a hard practice in Chicago before boarding the team flight to Vegas. Luke Richardson was trying to reinforce the effort necessary to win board battles in the NHL, which the coaches felt was lacking at times against the Bruins.

After the skate, all the players looked tired but also energized. Nick Foligno talked about how that was where the bar was set for every practice in Boston during his time there. For Bedard, the hard work was fun and a reminder of what it would take to finish three complete periods against the really good teams they were facing early in his career.

The game in Vegas was an awkward 3:00 PM local start as the Golden Knights celebrated Nevada Day. After the bag skate the day before, the hope—the goal—was to have a better start. The opposite materialized as the Blackhawks allowed two goals to the Golden Knights in the opening four minutes. The undefeated defending champions were giving the Blackhawks all they could handle for the first half of the first period.

But after the mid-period television timeout, the Blackhawks came out with a renewed sense of purpose. Ryan Donato scored to get the Blackhawks on the board. Later in the period, Foligno won a puck battle and batted the puck around a defender with one hand to a steaking Bedard, who ripped home a shot for his third goal of the season. The game was tied, and suddenly Chicago had the momentum.

The Blackhawks battled injuries and penalty killing throughout the game but were able to force overtime. Chicago finally got a power play and converted on a great shot from Kurashev to win the game in OT. After all of the long, hard work, the Blackhawks picked up a big win—and ended Vegas' undefeated season.

After the game, Bedard talked about the things the players had taken away from the hard practice the previous day, as well as what they had learned about the Golden Knights after playing them just six days earlier in Chicago. For him, scoring was starting to come in bunches. But he wasn't thinking about his personal scoring.

"I haven't thought about [scoring] too much," he said. "I probably had more shots in the other games I didn't score, but [Foligno] made a good play there and I tried to get in the right spot."

Building off the team's most impressive win of the young season, the Blackhawks had a couple days off in Arizona before facing an equally young, building Coyotes team. Bedard and the rest of the team were able to briefly experience life on a college campus; the Coyotes' home rink, Mullett Arena, was shared with Arizona State. With college football and the Arizona Diamondbacks playing in the World Series that weekend, the Blackhawks were able to spend some time together bonding.

When the puck dropped on Monday night, the opening shift went as well as the Blackhawks could have hoped. Bedard ripped home his first shot of the game just 28 seconds into the contest to give the Blackhawks a 1–0 lead. With the goal, Bedard became the youngest player in NHL history to score a goal inside the opening 30 seconds of a game—yet another "youngest" accolade to add to his collection.

After Bedard's goal, the game went south quickly. The Hawks allowed eight unanswered goals to a team that was right next to them at the bottom of the Central Division stand-ings. The night before Halloween, the Blackhawks lost by a scary 8–1 score.

Speaking with the media after the game, veteran forward Nick Foligno said the quiet part out loud. The performance from everyone on the roster was poor, and the result reflected their lackluster approach.

"This is gonna be really weird to say this, but maybe it's a good thing [that loss] happens and we have five days to chew on it," Foligno said. "Because I hope our team understands how you have to respect this league.

"It's a bad feeling in here because we're talking about trying to grow this. That was a perfect example of not anywhere close to what we're trying to do."

The Blackhawks didn't have another game on the schedule between the Monday-night debacle in Arizona and hosting the Florida Panthers on Saturday night. Foligno was speaking as much to the players in the room as he was to the media; if the terrible loss could prove to be a learning moment, then the dividends could serve a purpose that outweighed the two points in the standings they left on the table.

Bedard finished the month of October with four goals and two assists. He led all NHL rookies in goals scored and all rookie forwards in average ice time per game (19:45). One of the two rookies who averaged more ice time than Bedard was his teammate, defenseman Kevin Korchinski. Only Minnesota defenseman Brock Faber averaged more than 20 minutes per game as a rookie in the season's open-ing month of play.

Richardson saw some ways Bedard was getting more comfortable with every game, adjusting his approach to the speed and physicality of the NHL level while learning how and where to let his skill show.

"I think [he's] figuring it out," the Blackhawks' head coach said after practice during the first slow week on the calendar for the team. "Once he goes one time through [the league] he'll start to see the kinds of teams he's getting and the types of matchups he'll get on the road compared to at home…. But I don't think he really cares about matchups. I think he just wants to go play. I think he thinks and has the confidence that he can beat anybody at a one-on-one—and he might be right."

Bedard acknowledged there were still aspects of the professional life where he was adjusting, but he once again reiterated that playing hockey is what he loves to do.

"You get more used to it all the time," he said. "It's a lot of fun just playing games every other day—basically it's the best. It's been good so far. Obviously you have to adjust to that, but we get treated pretty well. I think that's something you can get accustomed to, but definitely learning as I go."

And that's what made the ongoing evolution of Connor Bedard as an NHL player so fascinating. When the team was off for four days with only a couple practices—albeit tough practices—between the disappointing loss in Arizona on Monday and hosting the Florida Panthers on Saturday, he continued to work at his craft while, occasionally, reminding us that he's still a teenager.

After the team had a fairly hard practice on Wednesday, Bedard and Korchinski stayed out shooting and passing with each other for almost 45 minutes after the rest of the team was off the ice. Media stood around in the dressing room waiting for the two young centerpieces of the rebuild to arrive to speak with them about the struggle in the desert.

The following day, the team stayed off the ice and just worked out in the gym. But head coach Luke Richardson acknowledged on Friday that they had to force Bedard to stay off the ice. Friday's practice didn't afford Bedard the opportunity to shoot around on his own after the rest of the team because of a meeting. And the visiting Panthers needed the ice for a practice of their own.

Even while he was putting in all the extra work to get better, it seemed he was impervious to the grind. He was always looking for little aspects of his game to get better or faster. Even after he skated in four different time zones in his first nine career games, the luxury of the NHL was what he had worked so hard to reach.

Now he was working toward the excellence that he had expected from himself at every previous level of his journey in the game. When the media would caravan across the dressing room and pile up in front of his locker like a traffic jam, he professionally answered every question in front of the bright lights and cameras. He was a polished media personality already.

But every once in a while, without a microphone on or a camera's lights in his eyes, someone would ask him about what music he listened to on his way to the rink on a game day, or what he thought of the food at the practice rink. And the young man who was still a young 18 would show his age, maybe only briefly, as he answered a casual question.

Bedard didn't have a set playlist of music for his pregame venture into the United Center. He preferred to mix things up on the drive. In the dressing room, he was in for whatever the team DJ selected for the night. He really was just one of the guys.

With the Devils coming into town and as he returned to the lineup from a shoulder injury that had cost him a week on the injured list, Taylor Hall was again asked about the comparisons between the two former No. 1 overall picks who were once his teammates in New Jersey—Jack Hughes and Nico Hischier—and Bedard. Hall initially broke down the differences in their styles of play and circumstances on each team when they arrived, but came back to Bedard seemingly having the weight of the world on his shoulders with the expectations that had been placed on him years prior.

That balance between answering questions and being available for the cameras and the microphones while still being a teenager living his dream and trying to get better was constantly on display behind the scenes.

How did he feel about his first month of the regular season?

"It's good," he said before hosting the Panthers. "It's gone quick, as well. We're…getting in the routine of getting in games. We're all chasing goals together [because] that's what we love to do. That's been a lot of fun. Everything's going pretty quick, so [I'm] trying to just take things day by day."

When the Blackhawks and Panthers took the ice, it was Chicago that effectively chased goals early and often. The Hawks put three goals on the board in the first period against the defending Eastern Conference champions, playing one of their more dominant periods of the entire season. The second period was nearly break-even with Florida playing a more desperate game, but there was only one goal scored.

Off Bedard's stick.

Bedard collected a loose, bouncing puck at his own blue line and attacked. Without a defender to break his rush, he ripped his patented wrist shot home and the crowd erupted.

As he skated past the visitors' cage, he raised his stick high in the air in his left hand and raised his right in a way many Blackhawks fans remember Dustin Byfuglien doing during the 2010 Stanley Cup championship run. It was as though he was asking the near-sellout crowd, "Are you not entertained?"

Chicago went on to win the game 5–2, a strong result for a team that had almost a full week to stew on its disappointing loss in Arizona. But the Blackhawks wouldn't have much time to enjoy their victory; the young, fast, and heavily favored New Jersey Devils were at the United Center the following night.

Earlier in the week, national media was hyping up the Devils–Blackhawks game as one between two of the league's bright young stars. Jack Hughes was leading the NHL with 20 points in his first 10 games. Many had compared Bedard to Hughes because of their stature and offensive ability before the draft, so this set up as a potential headline-grabbing affair.

But one thing the schedule makers couldn't predict was health. Hughes crashed into the boards and hit his head/neck on Friday night in St. Louis and wasn't available to play in the game on Sunday evening. New Jersey was also without its star second-line center, Nico Hischier, who—like Bedard and Jack Hughes—was a No. 1 overall pick. The storylines fans and media had hoped for weren't quite materializing.

Jack's younger brother, Luke, was one of the other rookies whom some considered a contender for the Calder Trophy as the league's top rookie with Bedard. And he was available for the game. After beating a good Florida team, Chicago was coming in confident against a banged-up Devils squad.

That confidence led to a great start. Taylor Hall scored 1:51 into the first period, and there were some in the crowd at the United Center who thought this night might turn out similarly to the previous evening. That would not be the case.

New Jersey scored the next three goals and won the game 4–2. Bedard's three-game goal scoring streak was snapped, and the effort from the Blackhawks was less than they expected after playing as well as they had against Florida.

After the game, the doors to the dressing room stayed closed for almost a full half hour. When the media entered, the room was quiet. The Blackhawks held a players-only meeting to clear the air and talk amongst themselves about the expectations they needed to have for each other and as a team.

"[We talked about] being accountable and playing in the systems that we've installed through training camp and the first few games of the season," Corey Perry said. "We do it in spurts, but we need to do it for a full game. We had a good heart to heart, and we'll move on."

"We have to [talk about it when we face adversity]," he continued. "That's a brotherhood. You're not putting anybody down. That's not what we're here to do. That wasn't the message. It's more being brothers and being able to talk about it and figure it out as men."

Head coach Luke Richardson, who appeared in more than 1,400 regular season games as a player, understood what the players needed to say to each other and was fine with them having that conversation amongst themselves. He gave the players the next day off after a tough back-to-back but made it clear to the media that if the Blackhawks wanted to improve, they needed to find consistency from one night to the next.

"I think it's important that we're all on the same page," veteran forward Tyler Johnson added. "We all play for each other. We're all trying to help each other. You don't want the season to go down a path that you don't like. We felt like we needed to stop a few things and address them. I think it's pretty important for everyone on the team."

For Bedard, hearing the veteran leaders on the roster clear the air and bring that accountability to the forefront after 11 games was a critical moment early in his rookie season that meant a lot.

"It's very important," he said. "I think what was said—I'll leave that to ourselves—but they've been around the league for a long time, and they know what it takes to win and what we need to do. As young guys we can soak up what they say, and I think that will be good for us in the long run."

The schedule was loosening up for the Blackhawks, who now had three days off before playing in Tampa. The team would travel to Florida to face the Lightning on Thursday and the Panthers—again—on Sunday. This would be a special trip for the team because it would be the team's Moms Trip. Each player could invite their mom or a special woman in their life to join the team in Chicago, travel with the team, and enjoy watching the team play with some special activities planned for when the team was preparing for games and playing.

"As close as people are to you, they still don't know your lifestyle and it's hard to explain it," Luke Richardson said after practice on that Tuesday. "Sometimes we complain about the schedule and travel and they come and see we're staying at the Four Seasons and on a private jet, they don't have any sympathy."

For Bedard, this was a fun time to reunite with his mother. Melanie Bedard flew into Chicago on Monday; Connor was looking forward to spending time with her and having her join the other moms in some camaraderie. After the team

practiced on Tuesday, he admitted he was excited that he
didn't have to cook for himself for a couple days. After joking
about FaceTiming with his mom while he tried to prepare
meals early in training camp, Bedard said his game in the
kitchen was progressing. Maybe just not as quickly as his
on-ice game.

"I've been pretty good lately," he joked about his cooking.

When asked if the menu might improve with Melanie in
town for a few days, he laughed, "It will be better than chicken
and rice."

Even with the mothers joining the team on this trip, the
game had additional significance. For the players, following
their meeting after the previous loss, this game presented an
opportunity to show their resolve and put together a good
performance.

It was also a potential revenge game for a number of players on both rosters. In the Blackhawks' room, forwards Tyler
Johnson, Corey Perry, Taylor Raddysh, and Boris Katchouk
had all spent time with Tampa. Perry had spent the previous
two years with the Lightning before agreeing to a deal with
the Blackhawks; the other three started their respective careers
with the Bolts. So there were still friends—and, in the case of
Raddysh, his brother Darren—on the other bench.

For the front office and coaches, the Tampa Bay Lightning
presented another measuring stick for the rebuild. Again,
when the Blackhawks hired Richardson, he and general manager Kyle Davidson spoke about Tampa (and Colorado) being
the two model franchises they were trying to replicate as they
rebuilt the Blackhawks. And this would be the first time this
version of the Hawks would face the Lightning with their
superstar-filled lineup.

Tampa came into the game having won two of their previous three. Star forward Nikita Kucherov was on a tear as well; he had four goals and seven assists in their three games leading up to hosting the Blackhawks. Some scouts and analysts had compared Bedard to Kucherov leading up the draft, so—like Jack Hughes—this was another star comparison on the schedule early in Bedard's career.

Chicago gave up an early power play goal and found itself trailing less than four minutes into the game. But then Bedard went to work, putting the first multi-point effort on his NHL résumé.

His first goal was impressive—and not how many had envisioned Bedard scoring in the league. Philipp Kurashev threw a pass across the crease, where Bedard was engaged in a battle with Tampa's future Hall of Fame defenseman Victor Hedman. Bedard was able to work himself inside Hedman and redirect the pass into the net for a tying goal.

What made this so impressive was not only Hedman's pedigree—six All-Star appearances, a Norris Trophy, and a Conn Smythe—but also the size differential. Hedman was listed at 6'7" and 244 pounds, meaning Bedard won the battle against a player who was roughly nine inches taller and 60 pounds heavier.

After Kucherov scored one of his patented goals to give Tampa the lead back, Chicago's other teenager—Kevin Korchinski—scored his first career goal to tie the game. In the final three minutes of the first period, Bedard set up Tyler Johnson with a no-look pass for a go-ahead goal and then executed a beautiful move to score his second goal with just eight seconds remaining in the period.

Bedard hadn't recorded a multi-point or multi-goal game to date, but he had two goals and three points in the first period against a team the Blackhawks organization viewed as a model they were striving to duplicate.

He added an assist on a Corey Perry power play goal in the second period and Chicago won the game 5–3. Bedard's performance made him the youngest player (18 years, 115 days) to record a four-point night in the NHL since Bep Guidolin did so on February 5, 1944 (18 years, 58 days). He also became the youngest player in Blackhawks franchise history to record a multi-goal game.

Another historic benchmark in what was becoming an increasingly impressive start.

After the game, though, Bedard's comments on the post-game show on NBC Sports Chicago weren't focused on his career-best performance. He first noted that he hoped three teammates who had left the game because of injuries—forwards Taylor Hall and Andreas Athanasiou and defenseman Jarred Tinordi—would be okay.

When pressed to talk about his own game, Bedard focused his response on his teammates again. "All of those were other guys creating stuff, and I was a beneficiary," he said.

His head coach smiled. "He's been here for a dozen games now; he's starting to really figure it out," Richardson said after the game.

The Blackhawks had some fun activities set up for the moms while the team practiced between games. The mothers of Corey Perry and Tyler Johnson, a couple of the veterans on the team, had never had a chance to go on a trip with the other moms on their sons' team. Perry said the trip was first-class across the board, and all of the moms were becoming friends. For a player who had been in the league for almost two decades, it reflected well on the organization that his mom and Connor Bedard's mom could hang out in a suite for a couple games and become friendly.

With the game against the Panthers starting at 1:00 PM ET, everyone's game-day routine was changed. Head coach Luke Richardson told the media before the game that he had gone to the gym in their hotel early in the morning to get in some work and spend some time with his thoughts. Soon after he got on a bike, he wasn't alone in the room any longer; Bedard had arrived to get in some pregame work as well.

The two both joked about the meeting after the game; Bedard said Richardson was "a horse on the Peloton" and noted that his work ethic is why Richardson was able to play the game for as long as he did. Richardson was impressed by Bedard's attention to detail and focus as well.

When the moms joined the team at the rink on the other side of Florida for the second game on the trip, there was buzz about Bedard's four-point game in Tampa. He added to the excitement with another highlight-reel effort in which he scored a couple gorgeous goals.

Bedard's first goal was all him. He took the puck away from a defender deep in the Florida zone and looked away from the net while shooting the puck top shelf against former Vezina Trophy winner Sergei Bobrovsky. On his second goal, Bedard fed the puck under a defender's stick on the rush and then reached over the stick to get his shot off. He was attacking on his left side of the net and the shot went in off the far side post.

After the game, Bobrovsky admitted he had nothing for the kid. He tipped his hat to the talented 18-year-old sniper who had individually created two incredible goals.

The internet and social media were on fire with the video clips of Bedard's two goals, even with NFL games overlapping with the 1:00 PM local puck drop. And the notes of his continued history-making performances were grabbing attention from the entire sports landscape.

At age 18 years, 118 days, Bedard became the youngest player in NHL history with consecutive multi-goal games. And Bedard's nine goals in 13 career NHL games were the most in Blackhawks history. No other player in the 98-year history of the franchise had scored more than seven in his first 13 games.

After the game, Luke Richardson spoke about his 18-year-old star setting the standard for the team's offense.

"As he gets more comfortable and we get more used to seeing that on certain nights we could maybe move him around to get other people going, too," Richardson said. "I mentioned before he just doesn't seem satisfied just getting his one goal every night. He's definitely looking for more. That hopefully becomes contagious in our team.

"He's got some special qualities. He's starting to find himself in this league and guys are learning how to play with him as well."

Foligno was asked about Bedard's goals and how he changed the game. Like his head coach, the veteran was complimentary of the skill that changed the game.

"Those are special. Both of them were great individual efforts," Foligno said. "That's what he does for you. When you play with a player like that—I've played with a couple, and we call them game-breakers. They either win you the game or keep you in a game like tonight where maybe we didn't deserve that. He's able to do it sometimes. The way he plays and his individual effort and his abilities—you appreciate that.

You don't want him to bail you out every night but those are the guys that can maybe get you a win you don't deserve."

Once again, Bedard's attention to detail and want to win showed when he spoke with the media. He was disappointed with the loss, talking about how the team wanted to start putting together consecutive wins; Chicago hadn't won two straight games yet in the season. Even after scoring a couple incredible goals, Bedard said he reflected on plays that could have gone in a better direction for himself and the team during the game.

Bedard saw his game growing as he spent more time in the NHL and played against veteran players more. But was that development natural—that he would get more comfortable with the play over time?

"Hockey's kind of a natural thing for all of us," he said. "[Maybe] not natural, but we work so hard. For me, that's where my confidence comes from—how much time I put into this. How much I've dedicated my life to it. It's just going out there and being confident in myself to try to make plays, but smart plays."

When the Blackhawks returned home after a road trip that some outside the room felt was successful, veterans and Richardson talked about feeling like the game against the Panthers was one they could—should—have won. The team usually took a day off after traveling, but their upcoming schedule wasn't favorable for that Monday being an off day. Chicago hosted Tampa on Thursday before a back-to-back with travel on the weekend, so the team skated the day after their matinee loss in Florida.

Even though the weekend saw Bedard put up more historic numbers, he was still working on his game. From ice level you could see his displeasure every time a shot missed its intended mark. And the shots kept coming. As had become his routine, Bedard stayed on the ice well after the rest of the team was done and on their way home. In fact, on this day, Kevin Korchinski left the ice to fulfill a media obligation and then returned to get in more work with Bedard. The two teenagers were becoming good friends and putting in a lot of extra work to get better.

Because of their schedule tightening up in the coming days, the Blackhawks spent a day in the gym on that Tuesday. But after the Monday practice, Richardson was asked if he needed to lock the doors to the rink so Bedard didn't get on the ice. The Blackhawks' head coach laughed a bit and said he didn't have keys to do that, but also noted that the work was how Bedard was continuing to improve seemingly every game and every practice. At the end of the year, the coach was confident that the young players on his team would have a better idea of how physically demanding the 82-game regular season could be, but at this point he was trying to make sure they found balance with time off the ice as well.

The night before Chicago hosted Tampa—without the Blackhawks playing a game to talk about—Wayne Gretzky was asked about the start of Connor Bedard's career during the studio show on TNT. The greatest of all time had some impressively complimentary things to say about Bedard's first 13 games.

"With young players, one of the hard things is you always tell them, 'You got to shoot the puck, you got to shoot more,'" Gretzky said. "Young guys don't want to be called selfish on the hockey club. You want to show your teammates, 'Look, I'm not a selfish player.' And he's not a selfish player. He sees the open man, but he doesn't hesitate to shoot the puck. I think he stepped in nicely, and he's been everything that everybody thought he was going to be.

"And he might even be better than we thought."

One week after facing Bedard in his own barn, Tampa Bay head coach Jon Cooper was in Chicago to face him again. That first experience was not a pleasant one for him or his team; Bedard had put four points on the board. But Cooper was in a unique position to speak about the skill that Bedard put on display because he's been around and coached some incredible players in his own right. Cooper led Tampa Bay to back-to-back Stanley Cup championships in 2020 and 2021 and a third straight Stanley Cup Final in 2022. He's been fortunate to have superstars like Steven Stamkos, Brayden Point, and Nikita Kucherov on his rosters.

Before the two teams took the ice, Cooper was complimentary of the young star, even if he had to joke at his own expense a little.

"I didn't get to see him very long, and every time I did see him he was lining up at center ice for a puck drop because he had either scored or had an assist," Cooper laughed. "You can tell he's extremely gifted. I love watching guys like that— they're special players in the league and he's got some special gifts. I'm sure he'll be the first one to tell you he's got a long way to go in this league. For me, you can't give NHL players time and space, especially guys that have those offensive gifts. We gave that to Connor in the last game and he burned us. That's a sign of a lot of hope for the [Blackhawks] franchise because when you start putting that word 'special'—I'm not saying that now, but he's well on his way to doing that with the gifts he has.

"You know, Connor McDavid is a different player than [Nikita] Kucherov. They're brilliant in their own ways. I would say Bedard has that vision Kucherov has. Again, small sample size for me. He's so young you don't want to anoint guys—I'm not a big believer in that—but he has the traits, and you can see it in his vision. You could see in some of the plays that he made. It's impressive at such a young age."

Cooper, who left practicing law to coach hockey, has always had a wonderful sense of humor about him but has also rarely minced words. He has no problem getting to the point quickly, and doing it with a smile and also an analytical edge. When he spoke about that "it" factor that he saw in Bedard—like Kucherov—he was pointed in his comments. Can a player learn the vision that players like Bedard and Kucherov have?

"If it was learned over time then everybody would have it," he said, smiling again. "There are only certain players who have that. They're playing in the best league in the world and they're so far ahead of other guys. You learn in situations, but it's a gift. That's why they're the best. Somebody has to separate themselves, and the gifted ones usually do. And the really gifted ones have the work ethic. That's what separates them. There are other gifted players that have those abilities but never make it because they don't have the work ethic."

After complimenting Bedard for a few minutes, Cooper hoped his team had a better answer for him than they had the previous Thursday.

One of the players tasked with containing Bedard for the Lightning was one of the best in the business, Victor Hedman. Bedard squeezed himself into position to score a goal in front of Hedman in Tampa, which raised a few eyebrows considering the size difference between the players; Bedard is a haircut under 5'10" and 185 pounds, while Hedman is listed at 6'7" and 246 pounds.

The game in Chicago played out in Cooper and Hedman's favor, thanks in large part to the former Norris Trophy and Conn Smythe winner. After a dominant performance in Tampa one week prior, Bedard was limited to just one shot on net and no points and was minus-two in the game. The Blackhawks lost 4–2 even though the game was tied early in the third period.

It was clear that Cooper's message to his team was to respect Bedard's ability—and take away any chances he might have to score. Tampa pressured Bedard's line constantly, and forced them to play the defensive end of the ice.

Hedman scored the game-winning goal. After the game, he complimented Bedard but also pointed out that the more he succeeded in the league, the harder it was going to get for him.

"We didn't give him the puck this time," Hedman said. "He's a special player. He gets treated like that and he's 18 years old, but he's gotta go up against the other team's shutdown line and their top D pair. It's not an easy league to come into. He's done a phenomenal job, considering the pressure on him. But he's got some good veteran guys around him that take good care of him. Today we didn't give him chances. He had to earn them. But you can still see when he gets the puck you don't know what he's going to do. Obviously, he did well against us before, so we wanted to make sure we were better against him today."

The Blackhawks' next two games were on back-to-back days against two teams that, at least on paper, were the first "easy" teams Chicago had faced to date. A Saturday matinee in Nashville, followed by a home game on a Sunday evening against the Buffalo Sabres, both of whom were hanging out near the bottom of the league standings with the Hawks.

Nashville followed the lead of the Lightning and boxed in Bedard most of the day. He saw two bodies skating at him the moment he touched the puck or entered the offensive zone for most of the first two periods. The one time he did find some open space, Seth Jones made a nice pass to him across the offensive zone for a quick one-timer on net. Kevin Lankinen made the save for the Predators, but Philipp Kurashev tapped in a rebound for the Blackhawks' first goal.

Bedard started to show some frustration with the number of whacks he was taking all over the ice—and some extra-curricular pushing, shoving, and holding that he was sub-jected to during the game. In the third period, his line with Kurashev and Nick Foligno was flying and had a few good scoring chances. Unfortunately, the Hawks were held to two goals on the afternoon while allowing four and the losing streak reached three games.

A quick flight home from the home of country music had the Blackhawks ready to face the Buffalo Sabres on their home ice on Chicago's Hockey Fights Cancer night. What made this game unique, at least on paper, was five former No. 1 overall picks taking the ice in the game: Bedard and Taylor Hall for the Blackhawks against Rasmus Dahlin, Owen Power, and Erik Johnson for Buffalo.

The Sabres came into Chicago ranked 31st in the NHL in faceoff percentage; the Blackhawks were 32nd out of 32 teams. And what had been a promising team over the summer with playoff aspirations was now struggling badly enough that Buffalo found itself in last place in the Atlantic Division and riding a three-game losing streak of its own.

Once again, Chicago found itself tied in the third period but came up short in the end. Bedard had an assist on a Philipp Kurashev goal, but the Blackhawks suffered a 3–2 final. For the first time during the regular season, the Blackhawks moved another young forward, Lukas Reichel, up to skate on Bedard's line. "We just thought we'd try the young guys together and see if there was a little bit of chemistry there," Richardson said about making the move.

As the media entered the Blackhawks' dressing room after the game, veteran Nick Foligno was available to speak. His locker stall was right next to Bedard's, and the young center was still getting undressed as the media surrounded Foligno. While Foligno spoke about the team searching for consistency and trying to learn the effort it takes to win in the NHL, Bedard was finishing putting his gear in a bag to move over to the team's practice rink that night.

Bedard wasn't happy despite putting another point on the board; he was up to 15 points in 16 games and won four of his 10 faceoffs that night. As Foligno spoke, it was clear that Bedard was listening while collecting his equipment. He was now roughly 20 percent of the way into his first NHL season and every night was a learning experience. But Bedard wanted wins more than points, and the team's losing streak reaching four games wasn't sitting well with anyone on the roster.

The Blackhawks had only won one of their first six home games. While Bedard listened, Foligno spoke about wanting to make the United Center a hard place to play for visitors again.

"I've been on the other side of it when you come in this building, and you're hoping to get a win some nights," he said. "I want to create that again. The fans deserve that. They sell it out every night to watch us play. It's a great building when we're playing the right way and we haven't gotten the results we need and it's disappointing because we want to make this a hard place to play. We talked about that at the beginning of the year, we want to make this a hard place to play and that hasn't been the case and that has to change. We're digging a hole here and we've got to find a way out of it because this is awful. This sucks."

For his effort in the two most recent losses, Bedard was as critical as he had been throughout his rookie season. "Nashville was alright. I thought I kinda sucked against Buffalo. We've got to get some wins here. It's obviously frustrating losing. [In] all those games, we're right there."

There were some games that felt close for the Blackhawks, and others that felt like the team was still a ways away from competing. And while everyone—the front office, coaches, players, and fans—recognized this season in Chicago was focused on development, there were hopes and expectations inside the room that there would be better results in the first 16 games of the season than only five wins.

CHAPTER 5

DRAMA

THE WEEK OF THANKSGIVING in the United States shaped up to be an interesting one for the Chicago Blackhawks. The night before the holiday, the Hawks were set to skate in Columbus before hosting two weekend matinees against the Toronto Maple Leafs on Friday and the division rival St. Louis Blues on Sunday.

The game in Columbus was circled on the calendar by many fans and media folks because it would be the first time we would get a chance to see Bedard and his World Junior teammate, Adam Fantilli, on the ice against each other. Fantilli, the third overall pick in the 2023 NHL Draft, starred at the University of Michigan for one season before signing his entry-level contract with the Blue Jackets.

Bedard and Fantilli were two of the elite players at the top of the draft, but were also friends. Before the game, the two sat down with radio voices for their respective teams—Troy Murray from Chicago and Jody Shelley from Columbus—for a joint interview. The teenagers shared a few jokes; Fantilli admitted to mistakenly touching Bedard's stick before a game, which is something Bedard takes very seriously. They also talked about the life of an NHL player being so much better than playing junior or college hockey.

While those two were sitting down to talk about their friendship and differing paths to the NHL, there was some drama in the background for the Blackhawks. Veterans Taylor Hall and Corey Perry both made the flight to Columbus, but neither was available for the game when the team took the ice for pregame warm-ups. Hall had flown back to Chicago to have his right knee examined, while Perry was simply listed as unavailable.

Coming into the game, Columbus had lost its previous nine. From the outside, there appeared to be a lot of friction between some of their players and coaches; Patrik Laine had been a healthy scratch in the week before Chicago's visit and expressed his displeasure to the local media. But with the Blackhawks down to just 11 available forwards, they were forced to skate seven defensemen in the game.

The result: an ugly 7–3 loss for the Blackhawks. Chicago was down 3–0 before Bedard scored late in the first period. A four-goal second period for the Blue Jackets put the game firmly out of reach. The game was the worst performance collectively of the season for the Blackhawks.

After the game, Blackhawks head coach Luke Richardson would only say that Perry was away from the team as an organizational decision. He didn't know or say anything else.

The team flew home to Chicago and took the ice on Thanksgiving Day for a tough skate after the bad loss. Before the skate, the team announced Hall was having season-ending surgery on the ACL in his right knee. The former No. 1 overall pick had been brought into Chicago to be a mentor for Bedard but also to help a team that didn't have much offense.

After only 10 games—in which he scored twice and added two assists—Hall's season was over.

Perry was also absent—completely. He didn't show up at the rink, and the questions kept coming, now directed at players in the room as well as the head coach. And none of those answering the questions knew anything.

"I'm not going to speak on it too much," Bedard said after practice on Thanksgiving. "Obviously it sucks he's not here, but we don't really have too much information on it or anything yet. But of course, he's a big part of the team and it sucks he can't be here today."

Both Richardson and Foligno said the same. Perry's absence was a decision that came from over their heads.

The noise surrounding the Perry disappearance was only further complicating an already stressful situation for the Blackhawks. They had lost five straight games—the last three of which were the first games on the season schedule against teams without deep playoff aspirations since the game in Montreal. This was supposed to be when the schedule was getting relatively easier for the Blackhawks, but their performances were seemingly getting worse.

And yet, Bedard was still working hard and appearing to have fun. He did say earlier in the year that he liked hockey, but the fact that he was still working hard and applying what the coaches were teaching during drills after tough, physical games was impressive. It was also noticeable that every time the Blackhawks had a home practice there were fans in the stands to watch him. School days, holidays, weekdays, and weekends, there were fans in the stands at the Fifth Third Arena a couple blocks from the United Center to see the new superstar—even during practice.

When he could, Bedard would take time to share a moment with some of the young fans who were clamoring for his attention. He would wave through the glass or flip a puck into the stands, and every time it made the young fan light up like a Christmas tree. That consistent willingness to participate in the engagement between players and fans wasn't lost on veterans on the roster. Nick Foligno saw the future of the Blackhawks—indeed, the NHL—in the great hands of Bedard.

"After every game, there's somebody that wants to meet him. Some kid from some other team, it could be anybody—it's hilarious actually how many people come out of the woodwork just to bring their kid down to him. He always has time. Whether he's in a good mood or a bad mood, he just goes over and makes that kid's day.

For some of those kids, that might be the only opportunity they ever get to meet somebody like that. For him to be selfless like that, it speaks volumes about him as a person and how he understands his role in this league. It's a great sign for a guy that's going to play for a lot of years."

After flipping pucks up to the fans and answering questions about veterans missing from the lineup, Bedard was able to get in a decent night's sleep before facing one of the players he modeled his game after for a second time: Auston Matthews was coming to Chicago on Black Friday.

When Bedard faced Matthews the first time in Toronto, the Blackhawks came away with an unlikely win in their third game of the season. Chicago had only won three times since then, and the Leafs came in playing well. William Nylander had a point in every game of the season and Matthews was near the top of the league in goal scoring once again.

With the game starting at 1:00 PM in Chicago, there wasn't a normal morning skate. Luke Richardson spoke with the media a couple hours before puck drop and the focus was once again on the status of the missing Perry. He was still out, and that's all the head coach knew about his veteran leader.

For his part, Toronto head coach Sheldon Keefe spoke briefly about how the Leafs had seen Bedard grow as a player since their first meeting early in his career.

"[Scouting Bedard] hasn't changed a lot from our perspective," Keefe said. "The strengths of his game remain the same as what we saw in the early going, which is dominant through the neutral zone and on the rush. He's got some guys playing around him who have similar strengths—they can bring the puck up the ice and can feed him and all those kinds of things. I'm sure his confidence is in an even better place. Clearly he'll be an area of focus for us tonight."

Bedard was becoming a focus of opposing teams' game plans. Beginning with the loss to the Tampa Bay Lightning in Chicago, teams were sending multiple players at Bedard as soon as he got near the middle of the ice, whether he had the puck or not. When Tampa head coach Jon Cooper said they couldn't give Bedard any space, it appeared the entire league heard his words and saw how his defensemen applied that focus.

The Lightning had held Bedard without a point in that game—after he torched them for four points the prior week—but he was able to put a point on the board in the three games between that game and hosting Toronto. The question was how, without Hall or Perry, the Blackhawks could muster enough offense to compete with one of the highest-scoring teams in the league.

The game against Toronto was a sellout. More than 20,000 fans—many in blue-and-white Toronto sweaters—packed the United Center in the middle of the day for what turned out to be an exciting game. Bedard was held off the score sheet through 60 minutes, but Toronto-area native Jason Dickinson recorded his first career NHL hat trick. Dickinson accounted for all three Chicago goals in regulation; Bedard was on the ice for all three of Toronto's goals and the game headed to overtime.

In the final minute of overtime, Bedard jumped on the ice with Kurashev and Korchinski. A furious 30 seconds followed, with the three young players cycling around the zone trying to find an opportunity to end the game. Finally, Bedard ripped a shot that went over the top of the net, popped up in the air, and came down, bouncing, on top of the net. The puck bounced over the crossbar and behind the Leafs' goaltender. Kurashev and Korchinski crashed and Korchinski tapped in the loose puck to end the game—and the Blackhawks' losing streak.

Korchinski saw the puck go in and sprinted to the side of the ice to throw himself into the glass in celebration. He was quickly joined in an embrace by Bedard—and then the entire team emptied the bench and celebrated with the two teenagers in the middle of it all. The visceral release of joy wasn't exclusively on the ice; the fans in the building were electric the entire game. It was loud in the United Center like it was 2015. And the young future stars of the team came through in the clutch.

The postgame celebration was brief. Korchinski had to leave the dressing room and compose himself in the hallway in the bowels of the United Center to do a television interview.

The team would practice the next day, but getting back in the win column was a desperately needed distraction.

When the team arrived at its practice facility a few blocks from the United Center on Saturday of Thanksgiving weekend, there were fans in the stands ready to cheer for their new heroes. But one of those players was not with the team still. And Blackhawks general manager Kyle Davidson was finally going to speak with the media regarding the disappearance of veteran Corey Perry.

The hockey world was buzzing about what the circumstances were surrounding Perry's departure. Richardson and other Blackhawks players knew nothing. He had flown to Columbus with the team the day before Thanksgiving and was simply removed from the team environment before the game that night. And hadn't been heard from or seen since.

When Davidson spoke with the media on Saturday, he didn't offer much insight into what had happened or how long Perry would be away from the team. His initial media availability didn't help the social media swirling around the Blackhawks' unknown problem.

The Perry situation was in the background when the team hit the ice for another matinee on Sunday against the St. Louis Blues. Following one of their stronger efforts of the young season, the Blackhawks came out completely flat against their division rivals. Bedard was held without a point for just the third time in 10 games in the month of November and the Blackhawks lost 4–2.

Unfortunately for Bedard and his teammates, that had become the trend for the Blackhawks early in the season. Every time they showed a strong, complete team effort, they came out flat and lost the next game. After this loss, the Blackhawks' dressing room remained closed for an extended period of time as the players had another internal meeting to discuss their effort that night. Once again, it was Foligno speaking with the media about a team that was struggling to consistently bring a winning effort to the ice every night.

While Foligno spoke to the media with conviction, Bedard was still in the room getting undressed. As had been the case the last time the team's de facto captain spoke after a mediocre effort, he was clearly speaking through the cameras and microphones to his teammates as much as he was answering questions. And Bedard was in the room to hear most of it.

He wasn't happy about another loss, either. The schedule was just starting to get busy again for the Blackhawks, who were approaching the quarter mark of Bedard's rookie season. They had only three wins to show for the month of November. Bedard was visibly frustrated, again, as he put his gear away and left the room for the night.

Because the Blackhawks had games at least every other day for three weeks following the loss to the Blues, the team had that Monday off the ice. When they returned for a full-team morning skate before hosting the Seattle Kraken in the finale of their three-game homestand, everything appeared to be business as usual for the skaters on the ice.

The headline earlier that morning was Patrick Kane deciding to sign with the Detroit Red Wings. The future Hall of Famer and Blackhawks legend had been rehabbing from a hip resurfacing procedure earlier in the year after the Rangers were eliminated from the playoffs. He was now healthy enough to make a decision on his next home, and he went with the Blackhawks' longtime rival.

After the morning skate, Richardson spoke with the media about the effort his team was getting from its fourth line and any lineup changes that might come that night. Bedard was asked if, as a hockey fan, it would be weird to see Kane wearing a Red Wings sweater in the coming days.

Bedard said he couldn't believe the first quarter of the season was almost gone. He did say it felt like he was settling into more normalcy as the games continued to roll through the calendar, but time was flying by for the young star.

Again, this felt like a relatively normal morning in Chicago.

Roughly an hour after the morning skate concluded and the team had left the United Center, the Blackhawks announced the team was placing Perry on waivers with intent to terminate his contract because of inappropriate conduct.

Whoa!

Kyle Davidson, the Blackhawks' general manager who had brought Perry into the Blackhawks organization after being a hated rival for almost two decades so he could help establish a new culture, informed the players and coaches of the decision to move on from Perry. He made it clear to his players that there was a standard of conduct that was not only expected but mandatory for employees of the organization moving forward. But he did not tell the players any specifics surrounding Perry's actions that led to his contract being terminated.

Davidson held an emotional press conference that afternoon to provide the media and public at large with some additional details as to why the Blackhawks were making the bold decision to release a former MVP.

"First and foremost, I want to start off by reiterating the organization is committed to a culture of accountability and upholding our values across our employees and players both on and off the ice," Davidson said to begin the press conference. "Last week, management was notified of possible misconduct by Corey Perry. We immediately pulled him from the game and conducted an internal investigation. Upon learning the findings of the investigation, we made the decision to terminate his contract.

"As this is an individual personnel matter, I will not be able to disclose any details related to the initial reporting, investigation, or the findings.

"However, I do want to be very clear on this one point: This does not involve any players or their families, and anything that suggests otherwise, or anyone that suggests otherwise, is wildly inaccurate, and frankly, it's disgusting.

"This has been a tough situation and I understand you wanted answers. It was important that we took all the necessary steps before sharing more. I hope you can understand that I may not be able to answer everything today, but I am going to be as open and honest as I can be, given the situation and out of respect for those involved."

The reason Davidson needed to emotionally, emphatically comment about players or their families with respect to Perry's dismissal was because of a rumor on social media suggesting Bedard's family might be somehow involved in the cause of the contract termination. A baseless lie grabbed traction in the ugly sides of social media as fans who still harbored ill will against the Blackhawks organization because of their inaction regarding the Kyle Beach situation were now taking it out on an entirely new front office and group of players—and focusing it on Bedard.

In the hours between Davidson's press conference and the start of a home game against the Seattle Kraken, social media was still buzzing with reaction to the news. The Blackhawks made a fairly surprising trade just minutes before the game started at the United Center, acquiring forward Anthony Beauvillier from the Vancouver Canucks for a fifth-round pick.

By the time the game started—12 hours after word broke that Kane was signing with Detroit—it had already been an exhausting day. But there was still a game to be played. And the players had to put their emotions after learning of Perry's formal departure—and the ugly internet rumors—aside for a couple hours and play a game that mattered in the standings in front of a near-capacity home crowd.

The Blackhawks took a two-goal lead in the first half of the opening period, but went to the dressing room tied after 20 minutes. The trend of not being able to hold a lead once again appeared.

Chicago scored twice in the second period and held that lead to the second intermission. Seattle was able to get one goal in the third period, but the Blackhawks held on for an important win in front of their home fans.

They needed a win in any way. After the game, it was once again their de facto captain, Nick Foligno, speaking to the media on behalf of the team. This time, he had to address not only a strong overall team performance but also the Perry situation.

"It's a hard day," Foligno said after the win. "It doesn't make it any easier because we care about Corey a ton, and we're going to wish him well. But our job here is…to galvanize around this, make sure we're holding ourselves to a high standard and understand how serious the Blackhawks are about that and the culture they want to build here. And we're lucky to be a part of it."

Two days later, Perry released a statement in which he, too, made it clear that the cause for his termination was his actions—which were amplified by alcohol in the situation in question—and had nothing to do with any players or their families.

When the Blackhawks took the ice in Detroit on Thursday evening, just hours after Perry released his statement, the conflicting noise surrounding the game and the organization was surreal. Between the Perry situation and Patrick Kane—one of the best players in the history of the Blackhawks and the only other player ever selected first overall by Chicago—being in the building as a member of the Red Wings, it was a unlike any night in recent memory for the organization or Blackhawks fans.

The game became a perfect storm for Chicago. Detroit was energized by the addition of Kane and came out of the gates flying. The Blackhawks had another flat performance following a strong game and lost 5–1. Bedard had an assist on Chicago's only goal of the evening.

As Bedard's success continued, players on opposing teams' kids were having the same reaction as Foligno's kids had when he was traded to and signed with Chicago. After the game in Detroit, Red Wings forward David Perron shared a photo on his social media of his son with Bedard after the Blackhawks' morning skate. The caption read: "Getting pulled out of school mid day to go meet one of your idols! Thanks for your time Connor".

Perron, a 35-year-old with more than 1,000 regular season games under his belt at the time, could have brought his son to meet his new teammate—future Hall of Famer Patrick Kane. But it was Bedard who was "one of [his] idols."

This was another example of the maturity being displayed by a player who was, still, only 18 years old. Bedard had come into the NHL with more fanfare and hype than any player in the history of the league. He was setting records and almost nightly was becoming one of the youngest players in the history of the league to do something. And while he was performing so well on the ice, he was also now dealing with being inundated with social media harassment of himself and his family based on a disgusting lie.

But he still had time to smile for a photo with fans—even children of opposing players—and hand sticks and pucks out to fans with signs begging for a glimpse of the new hero in the league. The juxtaposition of the pressure of being in the spotlight constantly while dealing with all the new negativity with his smile in social media photos and posts was striking. And it was consistent.

Even with statements from the organization and Perry saying the rumors around the Bedard family were lies, there were still dark areas on social media bringing it up. Thankfully, there were games every other day at this point on the calendar to take their minds off everything going on off the ice.

On December 1, the NHL announced Bedard was the league's Rookie of the Month for November. With all the noise surrounding the Perry situation, Bedard had still produced 12 points in 12 games to lead all first-year players. He became the first Blackhawks player to be named Rookie of the Month since Dominik Kubalik in 2020. The last Chicago player to earn the distinction before that? Kane, in 2007.

In the press release, the NHL noted Bedard had a point in seven straight road games, which was tied with Sidney Crosby, Steve Yzerman, and Sylvain Turgeon for the second-longest

streak by an 18-year-old. Colorado's Nathan MacKinnon registered a point in 16 straight games during the 2013–14 season.
The streak also tied the Blackhawks' record for longest by a
rookie, which was set by Darryl Sutter in 1980.

The Blackhawks were hoping the dust from the Perry inci-
dent could eventually settle as they traveled to Winnipeg for
a Saturday afternoon game. The team practiced with newly
acquired forward Anthony Beauvillier for the first time on
Friday, and he was immediately on Bedard's line and the top
power-play unit. Ordinarily, a player jumping straight onto
the top line in his first practice would get a lot of attention. Unfortunately, it was the Winnipeg media that drew
the ire of many of their colleagues and those who cover the
Blackhawks.

Bedard was asked repeatedly about the rumors—which
both Blackhawks management and Perry had stated were
lies—by Paul Friesen, a writer for the *Winnipeg Sun*. It was
the first time that Bedard had been awkwardly pressured by
media members to speak about the baseless accusations, and
a couple reporters in the scrum pressed hard. Even some local
members of the Winnipeg media questioned the ethics of
their approach, but Bedard answered the questions. Even if
he clearly didn't want to answer them, he kept his cool and
answered over and over again.

"[When] you've got the attention on you, stuff's going to
happen," Bedard responded to the first question. "Whether
you did nothing or you're not involved in the situation at all,
somehow it's all about you. That's not fair, but that's how life
works."

"I don't need to answer any more questions about this
stuff," he answered the second question, trying to shift the

subject back to the next day's game. "Obviously, it's all just a bunch of BS on the internet. It's of course [had] an effect on myself and my family, but who cares. It's out of our control. And it's all just fake, made-up stuff."

And yet, even after two strong answers, a third question came. His response: "It's whatever, like I said. Stuff gets out there, and people want to make jokes. Obviously, what happened with [Perry] is serious, and the first concern is he's OK and his family [is OK]. It's not great, but it's out of our control. I don't need to talk too much further on it."

Many young players would have wilted under the line of questioning. It would have been completely understandable if he'd simply said, "I'm not commenting on that any further" and moved on completely. He could have walked away and ended the media session completely. Even though he was clearly frustrated by the line of questions, he still answered them until someone else in the scrum asked about a different subject.

Again, the maturity was clear from a player who had dealt with media scrutiny since his early teenage years. In the first weeks of his professional career, Bedard was called out by a prominent Toronto columnist, Steve Simmons, after he wasn't made available to the media. Now, during Bedard's first trip to a Canadian Western Conference city, he was once again feeling heat from Canadian media members. Though this line of questioning left many questioning the writers' approach, it happened nonetheless. And Bedard stood tall.

In the wake of Bedard's answers to the questions in Winnipeg, elements of social media and Reddit started to awaken to the reality that the baseless lies were in fact having an impact on the lives of the 18-year-old and his family. There were few *mea culpas*, however. Because those rarely happen on social media.

However, one apology did happen—though not from the writer who asked the awkward questions. Mark Chipman, the executive chairman of the Jets organization, stepped onto the Blackhawks' bus after their practice and media session and quietly apologized to Bedard for the line of questioning from Friesen. Bedard didn't have to answer the questions, but he did. And Chipman took the step of personally making sure Bedard—the future of a division rival franchise—knew the Jets organization wasn't comfortable with the course of that day's media session.

Thankfully, there was a game on the schedule that shifted Bedard's and his teammates' focus to an opponent in spite of the surrounding noise.

Bedard was able to put that noise behind him quickly when he got on the ice. He scored the game's first goal less than five minutes into the first period to give the Blackhawks a lead. Unfortunately, the Jets were able to tie the game before the end of the period and add goals in the second and third periods to close the game with a 3–1 final score.

His goal extended Bedard's road point streak to eight games, meaning he now owned the second-longest road point streak in league history for an 18-year-old player, moving him past his idol, Sidney Crosby, and two others on the list.

Chicago didn't have much time to put the loss in their rearview mirror. The Blackhawks played the following afternoon in another matinee in Minnesota. Bedard would have to try to score against another former No. 1 overall pick, Marc-André Fleury. Fleury was the first pick in the 2003 NHL Draft and made his debut for the Pittsburgh Penguins during the

2003–04 season—which means Fleury had appeared in 21 NHL games before Bedard was born.

Once again, the Blackhawks' offense struggled to muster anything. Minnesota, who had made a coaching change earlier in the week because their season hadn't started the way anyone expected, dominated the game. Chicago didn't get on the board until the third period, when Taylor Raddysh batted a puck into the net on a power play.

Bedard was credited with an assist on the goal, extending his road point streak to nine games. Only nine rookies—not exclusively teenagers—in NHL history had a road point streak longer than nine games. Even with Chicago finishing the three-game road trip with only three goals scored, Bedard scored one of them and assisted on the other two. His ability to drive offense while the rest of Chicago's roster struggled was becoming increasingly impressive.

In the other dressing room, Fleury picked up his 548th career victory, moving him within three wins of tying Patrick Roy for second in NHL history. The Blackhawks fell to 7–16–0 on the season.

Coming back to Chicago, the Blackhawks were facing a stretch of four games in six days. The first game on that slate was a game against the Nashville Predators—their third consecutive game against a Central Division rival. When the Blackhawks played in Nashville on November 18, Bedard collected an assist on a Philipp Kurashev goal in the second period, but the Blackhawks lost 4–2. Chicago had won only twice in eight games since visiting Nashville.

Losing was not a good feeling for Bedard, even if the Blackhawks were doing a lot of it. With countries beginning to make preliminary roster announcements for the upcoming

World Junior Championship tournament, memories of his thrilling moments from two gold-medal performances still stirred Bedard. And he hoped to bring that level of excitement to Chicago in the future.

"At the end for everyone playing hockey [the goal] is to win a Stanley Cup," Bedard said. "That's what we're chasing here and trying to get better and build that culture. When you look back on tournaments or whatnot that you've won, you remember those feelings and it's pretty special, so you're always looking for that.

"I remember my 16-year-old year in [Regina], we didn't make playoffs and had a slow patch, kinda similar to what we've had right now at the start of the year. It was pretty slow, and we had a losing streak. It sucks, you never want to lose games. We know we're a better team than what our record shows. We've got to keep coming to the rink and being positive and trying to get better, and hopefully that shows in the win column."

It was somewhat strange that, coming home for four games in six nights, Bedard had only scored twice in his first nine games at the United Center. He had nine goals in 14 games on the road.

The Predators weren't likely to make it easy for Bedard to get one on the board. Juuse Saros came in playing well and was one of the better goaltenders in the entire league. While Bedard didn't score in regulation, his teammates beat Saros three times. Regulation ended with the score knotted at three, and the five minutes of free hockey didn't change that, so Bedard was on to the first shootout of his NHL career.

Bedard shot first for the Blackhawks. Over the previous two decades, that spot was generally reserved for Patrick Kane or

Jonathan Toews because they were nearly automatic over the course of their respective careers. The only other time Bedard had attempted a shootout goal against an NHL netminder was against Minnesota during the preseason. That did not go well; Bedard fumbled the puck and then got poke-checked and tripped by Marc-André Fleury.

This attempt went significantly better for Bedard. He buried the shot over Saros' left shoulder. Unfortunately, Nashville didn't miss on its first three attempts; the Blackhawks did not convert on the second shot and lost the game.

Picking up a point in the standings was a slight improvement from the Blackhawks' previous three games on the road, but it was still an unhappy room after the game. The Blackhawks felt like they had played most of that game well enough to win against a division opponent, but didn't quite finish. Veterans Nick Foligno and Seth Jones talked after the game about the missed opportunity to get back on the winning side of the ledger.

There wasn't much time for the Blackhawks to dwell on their mistakes or celebrate their successes. They were back on the ice for another game two nights later with the Anaheim Ducks in town. Both teams, despite playing poorly, were still generating plenty of buzz; any time the top two overall picks in the most recent draft face each other it's an exciting event. And Leo Carlsson was in Chicago to face Connor Bedard.

"[It's] very [exciting]," Bedard said before the game. "Obviously [Carlsson is a] special player and I got to know him decently well when we were in Vegas together for that Final game and combine, draft and stuff. Seems like a super nice, good guy. Getting to watch him this start of the season, what he's done has been incredible. I'm excited.... It was the four of us in Vegas. I knew [Adam] Fantilli from World Juniors and stuff, but with [Will] Smith and Leo, I didn't know them. It was good to get to know those guys and build that relationship. For both of those guys, it was fun to spend time with them and get to know them."

Richardson didn't send Bedard out for the photo op everyone wanted to start the game. There was no Carlsson-versus-Bedard opening puck drop. Richardson sent Jason Dickinson's line with Foligno and Joey Anderson out to begin the contest. Dickinson was quietly having the best start to a season of his NHL career and was being asked to shut down the opposing team's top line every night. In this game, Dickinson's line was tasked with handling the No. 2 pick from the summer's draft.

Dickinson performed his job exceptionally well. Carlsson won only two of 14 faceoffs in the game and put only two shots on net in almost 20 minutes of ice time. It was a stellar defensive performance from Dickinson, Foligno, and Anderson.

The story of the game, however, was Petr Mrázek. He completed his first shutout in nearly three calendar years—and he had to hold the Ducks to zero. The Blackhawks won the game 1–0 with their only marker coming off the stick of Kurashev.

On a second-period power play, Tyler Johnson got the puck to Bedard coming off the bench. It bounced a little on its way to Bedard, so he had to settle it down before pushing it into the center of the ice, where Kurashev was locked and loaded, ready to unload the shot that would prove to be the only goal of the night.

It felt good to win a game in front of the Blackhawks' home fans. Even if he hadn't scored a goal, Bedard was still happy to celebrate a victory.

Playing on home ice was something that players in Chicago had talked about being unique for generations. The ovation during "The Star-Spangled Banner" is something players on every team, not only the Blackhawks, talk about being special. With Carlsson in town for the first time, Bedard said the two spoke briefly after the game and the young Swede mentioned how cool the anthem was as a road player. Chicago's young star also noted that he wasn't taking that special moment for granted.

"I've just never really seen anything like that," Bedard said after the Anaheim win. "It's really loud, just how the fans get into it…. Everyone you talk to about playing here—as an away team or home team—that's one of the first things they say. It's pretty special and gives you goosebumps every time."

The locker room was loud on a Thursday night in early December after Mrázek's shutout win. But the task now was to do something the Blackhawks hadn't been able to do yet in the new season—win back-to-back games. Chicago hadn't won consecutive contests yet, something that was openly frustrating to every player in the room.

With only one night off between games again, the Blackhawks had a spirited practice on Friday. Chicago would host the St. Louis Blues on Saturday night and then the Washington Capitals on Sunday. Four games in six nights at this time of year was physically and mentally taxing for even disciplined veterans, and having the games made up of division rivals on either side of Carlsson coming in made it more demanding.

On Saturday night, the Blues were coming into Chicago after suffering a loss in Columbus the previous night. They were struggling, and the Blackhawks were waiting for them.

Chicago played one of its more complete games of the season in front of Mrázek again. A late short-handed goal for the Blues kept the Blackhawks from posting back-to-back shutout wins for the first time since 2017, but they were successfully able to get the monkey off their back and win two straight for the first time.

Bedard was surprisingly quiet in the game. He led Chicago with five shots on net, but won only one of four faceoffs in the game. After skating 22 minutes in the loss to Nashville to start the homestand, he skated 16 in the win against Anaheim and just under 17 minutes in the win over the Blues. Dickinson, who scored another goal, was taking ice time and pressure away from Bedard as the team started to find a groove offensively.

Richardson said Bedard's ice time being down wasn't any kind of load management for an 18-year-old in the midst of his first long NHL season, but more situational use and lead management for the team.

"I think he's been skating well and he's starting to get certain aspects of the game away from the puck," Richardson said. "He's obviously really good with the puck, but line matching at home probably plays a role in that. I'm not really watching his minutes too much. I think I threw him out once or twice to fill in a role when Reese was out for a shift in the penalty box and stuff like that.

"I think also games when they're close and we have the lead, we've been using guys like Dickinson's line and Tyler Johnson and Kurashev, guys who have more experience to play in a 5-on-6 situation at this level. He's probably not going to be part of that equation yet, but he's a great player and he has a good hand-eye coordination with stick abilities that, at some point, we'd like him to be involved in that. But right now, that probably plays into ice time as well at the end of the game."

Part of the Blackhawks' improved offensive play in the first three games of the homestand was the injection of Anthony Beauvillier into the lineup. Beauvillier, who was acquired from Vancouver a few hours after the Blackhawks announced they were terminating Corey Perry's contract, had played one game on the three-game road trip with the team. He couldn't follow the team from Winnipeg to Minnesota because he was still trying to get his visa issues cleared up so he could play for the Blackhawks in the United States, something that was "weird" to Bedard after having the veteran jump onto his line for just one game and then not be able to stay there the following game.

Beauvillier's visa issues were resolved before the Blackhawks started their home set. He traveled to Chicago late on Monday and played Tuesday with little rest. By Thursday, he felt like he was physically settling down from the movement following the trade. By Saturday, he felt a little more comfortable with his new linemates. Beauvillier scored his first goal with the Blackhawks in the win against the Blues on Saturday night. And Bedard's skill was grabbing his attention.

"Seeing him up close, it's definitely impressive what he can do on the ice at a high speed like he does," Beauvillier said. "And coming straight from juniors; I keep forgetting he's only 18 years. He clearly doesn't act like that. He's a pro already. He's working on his game. He knows what it takes to take care of his body. It's been fun playing with him. We just need to keep building chemistry."

Once again the music was blaring in the room after the game. The team finally celebrated a second straight win— and they did it on home ice. But they didn't have much time to dwell on this important victory, because the Washington Capitals were heading into Chicago the following night.

CHAPTER 6

LEARNING CURVE

I F THERE WAS SOME INCREASED LEVEL of interest around Bedard facing Leo Carlsson, the anticipation of Alexander Ovechkin being in the same game as Bedard was already percolating before the game against St. Louis the prior night. One of the game's all-time leading scorers, Ovechkin had scored a hat trick to reach 800 career goals in his trip into Chicago the previous year. On that night, he received a nice moment of tribute and an ovation from the crowd at the United Center and handshakes from both Patrick Kane and Jonathan Toews. This time, Bedard would be waiting for him as the young player many expected to be one of the next great scorers in the game.

Of course, the two players were asked about each other before the game. Ovechkin was complimentary of Bedard's wrist shot, calling it "tremendous."

"Yeah, I mean he's great. You can see the young guys come into the league and they're superstars, they're very talented players. It's fun to watch them play. I wish him the best of luck, just not against us," Ovechkin said with a chuckle.

For Bedard, another one of the game's icons whom he'd looked up to growing up was now going to be on the ice against him. As a player who grew up idolizing Sidney Crosby, the rivalry between Pittsburgh and Washington was one that he watched frequently. And the legendary scorer's ability to put the puck in the net was also something that stood out.

"You know, it's pretty exciting for me, first time going against [Ovechkin]. You know they've got a lot of good players over there but growing up I watched him a lot…. I think the biggest thing is him and Crosby's dueling hat trick game was pretty cool. That sticks out for me."

Both teams played the night before; the Capitals beat the Rangers in Washington before flying to Chicago, while the Hawks were able to sleep in their own beds following the win against the Blues. The first period of the game looked like two teams playing the second half of a back-to-back, with a few penalties and some sloppy play from both sides.

The Blackhawks got on the board first, with Bedard picking up another assist on a Kurashev goal. The first half of the second period saw the Blackhawks put good pressure on Washington. But the mental lapses that had haunted Chicago thus far in the season showed up again. The Capitals scored three goals in a little more than seven minutes to blow the game open.

A fourth Washington goal late in the third period put the game out of reach. But the Blackhawks kept fighting. Bedard rifled a few shots past the net on late power plays before flipping a backhand pass across the offensive zone to a streaking Connor Murphy, who scored the Blackhawks' second goal of the night. That would close the books on the scoring for the night.

Bedard finished with two assists—his first multi-point game since scoring twice in Florida against the Panthers almost a full month earlier—but it was obvious he really wanted to score a goal. He was stuck on only two goals on home ice still.

The final score was a disappointing end to a four-game homestand in which the Blackhawks finished 2–1–1 and played well in the first three games. As he left the ice most nights, Bedard would remove his Blackhawks sweater and pads to reveal shredded undergarments from the physical play during the game that night. The Washington game was no different. His undershirt was missing a sleeve as he slowly removed the remaining gear while the media asked Murphy questions about the game on the other side of the dressing room. He disappeared before the cameras moved across the room to speak with Foligno about the loss.

After the game, Richardson was asked about Bedard's game and the young player extending some of his shifts longer than the coaches might like in an effort to try to create more offense. Bedard had been on the ice at the end of one long shift when Washington scored its first goal of the night.

"I think you have to learn shift length in this league. And I think sometimes it's too long," Richardson said after the loss. "That's going to be a learning curve. He's used to being able to handle that but when you've got a guy—Mantha's a big man and has a sneaky, long stride and if he gets a half stride ahead of you, you're either taking a penalty nowadays or it's a scoring chance. It happened to be a scoring chance."

"I've talked to him before and he said, 'Yeah.' Sometimes I think he's so analyzing the game and looking around that he honestly doesn't realize how long he's been out there. So that's just the learning curve. He has to realize that in the NHL, no player is going to play a proper shift for two minutes in length and expect to do well at the end of it. And if you do, you're cheating out there. I think you need to make sure that you're constantly learning and building yourself up, especially the young players. We give them the information and hopefully they ingest that and figure that out."

The balance the coaches were trying to find with Bedard was part of that learning curve, something Richardson talked about frequently with Bedard and other young Blackhawks players. The head coach went on to compliment Bedard's offensive game that night, noting a few good shots that had just missed their mark and his ability to forecheck and take pucks away from opponents.

"Again, he's young and he's learning and he's eager. He wants to try to do well every night."

If skating against Ovechkin on home ice was an intriguing matchup, the Blackhawks' next game garnered attention from all over the United States and Canada. Chicago was in Edmonton to face the "other" Connor—McDavid. The best player in the game against the kid who was supposed to be the next…him.

McDavid, the No. 1 overall pick in the 2015 NHL Draft, came into the league with the "generational talent" label as well. Like Ovechkin and Crosby, he was tasked with shifting the course of his franchise's future—something not unlike what Bedard was facing in a post-Toews/Kane Chicago. But an injury cut McDavid's rookie season short and took him out of the race for the Calder Trophy as the league's rookie of the year.

With the anticipation of the McDavid–Bedard matchup coming already when the NHL's full slate of games on Sunday night ended, the media talking about the game was enormous. ESPN, which had the broadcast rights for the game, was promoting the game during its NFL shows on Sunday and before *Monday Night Football*. And nearly every outlet that covers hockey had a thoughtful long read on the matchup between players who many felt would eventually share more than a first name.

Mark Lazerus and Daniel Nugent-Bowman of The Athletic wrote a lengthy piece about the comparisons between the two Connors. In that story, Oilers forward Ryan Nugent-Hopkins, who was the No. 1 overall pick in the 2011 NHL Draft, remembered a workout outside Vancouver years prior in which a much younger Bedard had raised eyebrows of other established NHL players.

"We were like, 'Who's this kid on the ice?'" Nugent-Hopkins told The Athletic. "And then he was 13, and at 14 he was shooting the puck as hard as anyone on the ice already."

Ryan S. Clark and Greg Wyshynski at ESPN published a piece that asked other recent top picks their initial impressions of Bedard. They also spoke with some players who were teammates of players who had come in with lofty expectations. Chris Clark, who had played with Ovechkin in Washington as a rookie and was now director of player personnel for the Columbus Blue Jackets, noted that the attention for a player with the profile of an Ovechkin or Bedard extends well beyond hockey media circles.

"Every time he goes to a new city, it's not just going to be the hockey writers covering him. It's going to be the sportswriters and the entertainment people. More and more reporters—not just like the normal five hockey [writers] that are there every time," Clark told ESPN. "It's an event. Even if you don't like hockey, you've heard of him. It's an event."

Clark's memory of the media following Ovechkin was in parallel with Bedard, who dealt with a media swarm that doubled every time a team faced him for the first time. The expectation was that there would be a lot of additional media in Edmonton for Bedard's first game against McDavid as two of the most hyped prospects to ever enter the league as 18-year-olds did battle.

The two were familiar with each other on and off the ice already. They had worked out together for multiple years at the BioSteel Camp in the weeks before NHL training camps opened. Bedard admitted to watching McDavid as often as he could growing up and still since he joined the league. And McDavid was already impressed with Bedard's confidence from their time on the ice together at the camps. Speaking with Lazerus and Nugent-Bowman, he recalled one specific play from the camp the year before Bedard was drafted.

"There was a two-on-one, and he was looking off Sid [Crosby] and shooting the puck," McDavid told The Athletic. "He was 17 at the time. Obviously, he's got the confidence on the ice. I say that respectfully, not in a bad way."

Bedard's confidence remained evident through the Blackhawks' struggles to win games and a personal goal-scoring drought. There were moments throughout the season when it was clear he was more excited for a game and opponent than others; that's not to say he wasn't locked in for every game, but when Crosby or Ovechkin or MacKinnon was on the other side and there were more eyeballs on the game, Bedard wanted to elevate his game.

McDavid on the other side was the peak opponent for anyone in the NHL, but especially Bedard. And a national television audience in both Canada and the United States would see their first battle. Before the game Bedard was asked about skating against players like Sidney Crosby in his first game and, now, McDavid. His response was almost identical to what he'd said in Pittsburgh two months prior: during warm-ups he might look over and enjoy the moment, but once the puck drops it's time to play the game. But he was still in awe of what "the other Connor" was doing in the league. And he didn't want the game to be overwhelmed with the Bedard–McDavid storyline, even if that's where all of the media attention was focused.

"I don't think either of us would see it as individual head-to-head. It's our teams going at it," Bedard said. "For me, obviously watching him the past, I guess, eight years in the NHL and following him like any hockey fan before that, just what he's been able to do is just remarkable. So getting to see it up close here tonight and go up against it should be a lot of fun."

One strange part of Bedard's stat line to date was that his numbers were better away from the United Center. After a decent four-game homestand in which he had three assists, Bedard was still stuck on just two home goals and five assists in 13 games. He had nine goals and seven assists in 14 road games. The difference in production at home and on the road was a puzzle to his head coach as well.

"[Bedard has] had a couple of really big games on the road, for sure, in Florida and Tampa. But other than that, I don't know if there's any rhyme or reason," Richardson said. "We try to get our match-ups here, usually better. Nowadays, usually it was, I know in the old days, it used to be the homers, and everybody was a homer and make jokes about it, kind of razz that player on the ice. This is the opposite scenario. Really, I don't know what the reason is."

That trend continued for Bedard in Edmonton. On his second shift, he received a pass from Alex Vlasic as he entered the offensive zone, and he ripped his patented wrist shot under the stick of Mattias Ekholm and over the left shoulder of Oilers goaltender Stuart Skinner for the first goal of the game. McDavid had the primary assist on the Oilers' tying goal less than seven minutes later.

What everyone stayed up late into the night to see was happening early in the game—Bedard and McDavid were putting on a show and didn't waste much time in doing so.

ESPN put a mic on one of the Connors during the game, but it wasn't the 26-year-old superstar. Bedard was wearing one under his pads so the national audience in the United States could hear some of his interactions with teammates.

The Oilers pulled away and won the game 4–1, with Bedard's goal the only score for Chicago. McDavid had two assists in the game.

After the game, Bedard's demeanor was more subdued. He still hated losing. The Blackhawks played the game without their top defenseman, Seth Jones, who was injured. Kevin Korchinski was away from the team dealing with a family issue. And veteran defenseman Jarred Tinordi was in the concussion protocol. Even with four young defensemen with fewer than 100 combined regular season games on their résumés skating against a team with the offensive firepower, Bedard wasn't making excuses. He continued to compliment his teammates and talk about the faith they have in the room in guys to step up and contribute.

When asked about his goal—a highlight-reel moment that had the television networks in both the United States and Canada buzzing well after the game—he was tempered still.

"I just kinda shot and it went in," he said very matter-of-factly when asked about what he saw on the scoring play. He said he hadn't seen it on a replay yet and didn't really feel like it was anything special, even if the broadcasts and other players were in awe.

"That's a world-class shot right there," Jason Dickinson said after the game. "I think that's a play that he knows it's muscle memory, he knows his spot, he knows where he is, and he knows where the net is and he's just picking that spot and he's trying to make the goalie beat him. And sure enough, he won that one today."

After speaking with the media in Edmonton, the Blackhawks boarded a plane destined for Seattle, where Chicago would face the Kraken on Thursday night. Unfortunately for the tired and banged-up Blackhawks, the weather had other ideas. Their plane was diverted to Portland for the night (well, morning at that point), and the team then made their way to Seattle without their regular off-day skate.

The Kraken made the playoffs following the 2022–23 season and had the reigning Calder Memorial Trophy winner, Matty Beniers, in their lineup. When the season started, things were hopeful in the Emerald City. But a bad start fueled by injuries and inconsistent play had the Kraken near the bottom of the standings when the Blackhawks arrived. Two teams desperately needing a win; one tired from a lot of travel, the other coming off a win.

Seattle blitzed the Blackhawks right out of the gate, scoring three minutes into the game. The Kraken took a two-goal lead to the dressing room for the first intermission and a 5–1 lead to the room after two periods. The final score: 7–1 in favor of the Kraken, and Bedard's 10-game road point streak was over. Chicago's only goal came from Taylor Raddysh.

The loss was deflating because the effort wasn't there. Veteran forward Tyler Johnson used phrases like "pissed off" after the game to describe his personal emotion from the game. There was more going on around the ice than on the sheet that impacted the Blackhawks' play, however.

Alex Vlasic, who had been pressed into suddenly being the team's No. 1 defenseman because of injuries, left the bench for the second half of the third period. Chicago was down one-third of its opening-night lineup and was running on fumes.

When the dust settled from a bad loss, the team boarded their charter jet. But they weren't headed back to Chicago. Not quite yet. The Blackhawks flew to Saskatoon because the team—the brotherhood—needed to tend to one of its own.

Kevin Korchinski had been away from the team for more than one week to deal with an unspecified family matter. Sadly, his father passed away. And the funeral for Larry Korchinski was taking place on Friday. The entire Blackhawks team was going to attend the services to support their 19-year-old team-mate in one of the hardest moments in his young life.

It was an emotional trip for the team before returning to Chicago, and the schedule of practices and games continued to press onward. But it was time well spent as the players invested in each other and showed the Korchinski family that the Blackhawks family was with them.

"You don't want to use it as a rallying thing, but it makes guys realize how fortunate we are to play, and that, when real life hits, nothing else matters but your family," Nick Foligno said after practice the next day. "When a brother hurts, we all hurt. And we're playing hard for him [Sunday]."

"It's unimaginable what [Kevin] and his family are going through," Connor Murphy said. "We were grateful to be there to show support, offer condolences…[but] you can't put into words the pain you feel for them."

Head coach Luke Richardson was glad the schedule lined up for the team to have the ability to support Korchinski. "It was a sad day for everybody involved, but I thought it was really great that the schedule permitted us to be there to support Kevin and his family. It's a tough time. Hockey is always great like that, but sometimes the schedule gets in the way. So that was great for us to be there. I'm sure they appreciated the support."

The Blackhawks had more injuries to sort through when they got to practice. As the coaches tried to make roster decisions as best they could and start involving new players in special teams practices, they did so with heavy hearts. But the calendar wasn't slowing down. The highest-scoring team in the league would be in Chicago for a Sunday matinee whether the Blackhawks had a fully healthy roster or…what they had left at this point in the season.

This game was likely one of the first Bedard circled on the schedule when he looked at Chicago's 2023–24 season. Growing up just outside Vancouver, the Canucks were his favorite team "as a kid." Of course, coming from an 18-year-old, that statement made some media members chuckle, but now he was a Chicago Blackhawk, so the fandom had to be put aside. Still, playing his hometown team would undoubtedly have some extra significance.

Undermanned still because of injuries, the Blackhawks put up a valiant effort. Chicago scored the game's first goal and took a 2–1 lead early in the second period, but simply did not have the depth to beat the Canucks. In a 4–3 loss, Bedard was credited with assists on the Blackhawks' second and third goals and skated a new career-high 23:16. Part of the reason his ice time was so high in the game was yet another injury; forward Joey Anderson left the game after two periods because of a shoulder injury and did not return, opening the door for Richardson to give Bedard more ice time.

The head coach was happy with Bedard's performance, though the entire team had its share of mental and physical lapses in a second period that saw the Canucks score three unanswered goals.

"I thought he was doing some great things in the third period, so it was easy to do," Richardson said after the game. "We've had that conversation before where, take short shifts, do the right things, you can't do it all by yourself, not yet anyway. I think he bought into that tonight and he got to the bench and he was ready to go back out there and he's fresh. It's a good sign. He was very dangerous in the third period and at the end, and that's what we need from him.

"Just like everybody in the second period, [he was] trying to force it a little bit. We turned pucks over, as did he, but so did lots of other people in the second period. It gets frustrating and it gives the other team extra fuel. He played way better in the first, with lots of opportunities, and in the third. And that's how the team rolled, as well. It's a good lesson. We've got to make sure we play to 60 minutes and not change our style and sit back and protect just our zone, even though we didn't even have the lead."

Even with that critique of his star rookie, Richardson was pleased overall with the effort from what he had left of a roster. One-third of his opening-night lineup was not available for this game because of injuries, Perry's termination, and Korchinski still being away from the team. When asked about the mounting injuries, he joked that maybe he couldn't have as many practices just to keep his team as healthy as possible.

One of the unique qualities Richardson displayed during his first 18 months as the head coach of the Blackhawks was patience. When he was introduced as the team's head coach the summer prior to Bedard's selection, he joined an organization that was fully transparent with him as a candidate; it was going to rebuild, and times were going to be tough before the light at the end of the tunnel could be realized. He had signed up for this, even if he hated losing as much as his teenage phenom.

Even with the mounting losses the prior season and star players leaving the organization, Richardson was always positive about the direction of the team and the opportunities available for players who might be the next man up.

This season, though, hopes were that the veteran additions would lead to an improved product on the ice. But injuries and off-ice issues had stripped Richardson of the roster he thought he had when the puck dropped in Pittsburgh in early October.

As the season progressed and the wins continued to be rare, his focus remained on the development of his young players. Whether it was Bedard or Lukas Reichel up front or any of the half-dozen defensemen who saw action with fewer than 100 career regular season games played, his analysis of a player's performance was pointed on the effort and the learning more frequently than the box score.

He did give his team the day off following the loss to Vancouver, but they still found themselves collectively on the ice at the United Center for the team's winter holiday party.

Players brought their significant others and children along for an evening skate on the NHL ice in front of a barn that did not have more than 19,000 watching them this time. Instead, it was simply a fun time as the families of the players who were building a family together on the ice and in their dressing room had a casual skate together.

The team shared some video clips from the event on its social channels. Jason Dickinson had his young baby on the ice, and other players were teaching their little ones to skate. Bedard? What do you think he was doing? He was chasing Nick Foligno's kids around the ice in their hockey gear and Blackhawks jerseys, giving them a hard time as they tried to shoot the puck and handle it around him. His smile radiated like the top of a Christmas tree as he played big brother with his teammates' kids.

With all the stress of the season, being able to unwind for a few moments and invest in each other as people meant a lot to the players—as did spending the time to travel to Saskatoon to be with Kevin Korchinski at his father's funeral the previous week. When the Blackhawks took the ice on Tuesday morning for a pregame skate, one of the first skaters to emerge from the room was Korchinski. He had been away from the team for nearly two weeks to be with his family in an incredibly tough time. But he was now back in Chicago, getting his legs back under him so he could join the lineup again sometime soon.

Korchinski wasn't quite ready to be in the lineup with the Colorado Avalanche in town, but his presence in the room lifted the spirits of his teammates and coaches.

The two teenagers had spent a lot of time together since they were teammates at the World Junior Championship.

Frequently, when Bedard stayed out on the ice after practice to get in extra work, Korchinski was out there with him. Their bond as friends—and the collective future of the Blackhawks—was noticeable early in the season. And Bedard was noticeably happy to have Korchinski back with the rest of the team.

"[It's] good to have him here," Bedard said after the morning skate. "Obviously it's a very tough situation for his family and he's part of our family—one of our brothers—so [it's] good to have him. And I think it's going to be good for him being back in this environment and we're happy to have him back."

With Korchinski back with the team—but not yet in the game—there remained a very tough opponent on the schedule that evening. The Blackhawks concluded their season-opening road trip gauntlet with a thorough beating in Denver, the first time Bedard faced Nathan MacKinnon, Cale Makar, and a team the Blackhawks were hoping to emulate in the coming years. That game stood out in Bedard's memory as one of his first significant moments as an NHL player.

"I hope [I'm more prepared to deal with Colorado's speed]," Bedard said with a bit of a smirk and chuckle after the morning skate. "Last game against [MacKinnon] was hard. I think that was a pretty big welcome-to-the-NHL moment. I don't know if I got a puck touch, so hopefully tonight's better. They're a great team and obviously they won not long ago. They have guys like MacKinnon, [Mikko] Rantanen, and Makar. They have so many players like that, so it's fun to be able to go against some of the best teams."

MacKinnon's name frequently came up in the media when Bedard did something noteworthy statistically as a rookie or a teenager. Bedard's road point streak came up short of tying or passing MacKinnon's NHL record. And the leader of the Avs was on an MVP-level tear when the Colorado team landed in Chicago.

As those comparisons continued to be made, questions were frequently raised about how a player as young as Bedard could perform as such a high level—especially with the nightly scrutiny of the media and attention from opposing players and coaches. According to his head coach, Bedard was just built differently.

"There have been guys throughout the years that have done that, way before I played. There are special players that came in…when Gilbert Perreault came into Buffalo. He was one of the best skaters and an elite player for his whole career, from day one. Denis Savard was here, right? Great player and obviously lots of things to learn when you're 18, but still elite players offensively. They see the ice well, and they kind of can play in most situations and they do well almost their whole career. It goes all the way through Crosby, McDavid, now we're looking at guys like Connor doing it here again. We're just lucky we have him and we can work that team around that great skill and that great drive. I think the drive is just as important as the skill, and that's what makes these guys special."

That smirk and chuckle that came across Bedard's face when asked about being better prepared for MacKinnon was subtle foreshadowing from the teenager. When the puck dropped that night against the Avalanche, the Connor Bedard who showed up at the rink was a more confident player on a mission to make amends for his previous, disappointing performance against Colorado.

Bedard was flying right out of the gate. He was credited with the second assist on Chicago's first goal of the night, a play on which he took the puck away from an Avalanche skater in the offensive zone and flipped a pass through traffic clear across the zone to a streaking Nikita Zaitsev. Zaitsev's shot hit the post and was banged in by Ryan Donato on the doorstep.

After Colorado scored two unanswered power play goals—the second of which came with Bedard in the box—he once again drove the offense. This time he received an outlet pass from Donato for a 2-on-1 break. Bedard looked off the defender and goaltender and flipped a perfect pass to a streaking Lukas Reichel, who unloaded maybe his most confident shot of the season to score his first even-strength goal of the year. As Reichel pointed to Bedard in appreciate for the setup pass, Bedard confidently nodded his head.

Bedard started the scoring play that led to Chicago's game-winning goal in the third period, a power play marker from Tyler Johnson. He wasn't credited with an assist on the play, but Bedard now had two assists in each of his last three home games.

He finished the night with six shots on net in 21:52 of ice time, an eye-popping departure from the zero shots on net he had in Denver two months prior. In a game that featured some of the best players in the game on the other team, the player who had everyone's eyeballs the entire night was Bedard. After the game, his head coach talked about how impressive the performance was from his young forward.

"A lot of people have the talent, but not all the people have that drive. He remembers that and he probably didn't like that feeling. He wanted to show a better version of himself and our team, and I think he did that tonight," Richardson said.

As Bedard's game evolved and grew during his rookie season, there was an ongoing dialogue between the media and

Richardson regarding his time on ice. Richardson was asked after the Colorado game about how comfortable he was with Bedard having a few extended shifts; a couple were over two minutes in length. The head coach noted that there were now times when the team felt more comfortable with his instincts and him pushing for a scoring chance, but Bedard still heard from behind the bench when his attempt to create a scoring chance at the end of a long shift turned into a rush for Colorado in the opposite direction.

Richardson's ongoing focus was on the development of Bedard and allowing his instincts and ability to accelerate his learning curve while not putting him in positions where he might not be able to take advantage of a situation. The coaches were still, 31 games into the season, learning as much about what Bedard could do as he was learning about the game at the NHL level.

Even while he was learning the NHL and developing his game, Bedard's off-ice activities continued to fill his schedule. He was also getting used to being the face of the franchise and, in many regards, one of the faces of the NHL. Before the Blackhawks hosted the Avs, Canadian Imperial Bank of Commerce (CIBC) announced an endorsement partnership with Bedard on their social media channels and he attended a meet-and-greet with some of their employees in Chicago.

Before the Blackhawks practiced the day before hosting the Montreal Canadiens, the NBA's San Antonio Spurs were in Chicago to face the Bulls. This created the first opportunity for hockey's generational prospect who had been the first overall pick in the NHL draft to meet basketball's generational prospect. Bedard took a few photos, shot a few pucks in a practice area that was not on the ice, and had a conversation in the

Blackhawks' dressing room at the United Center with Spurs center Victor Wembanyama. The photos made clear which one of the two teenagers played which sport; Wembanyama is 7'4", making him 18 inches taller than Bedard.

"It was pretty cool," Bedard said about meeting Wembanyama. "Obviously [he's] a great face playing in the NBA. He's going to be—or he already is—really special. Getting to talk to him a bit and hear his perspective, coming over from Europe and [being in] similar situations—him even more just with how big the NBA is. It was good to get to talk to him."

The two swapped signed jerseys and talked for a few minutes. Wembanyama, who was born and raised in France, said he liked to watch hockey and when players dropped the gloves. Bedard informed him that he wasn't a fighter. The basketball star was learning to like the game on ice. And this meeting made for a lot of buzz on social media as the two players many had tabbed as the next great players in their respective sports enjoyed a few moments together.

As the season progressed, the requests of Bedard for media opportunities, sponsorship requirements, and other moments continued. They weren't as frequent or time consuming as the media tour he embarked on before training camp, but it was still noticeable how frequently he was showing up in various situations. Bedard said it wasn't a very big deal, though; he was still just enjoying being an NHL player.

"It's not a very big price to pay," he said. "At the start of the year, there was a lot of stuff I was doing, so I was getting a little tired. But it's been good. I'm OK to answer a few questions here and there. I don't mind too much. I get to play here, so I can't really complain."

Over the final two days of the schedule before the NHL took its leaguewide three-day break for Christmas, the Blackhawks hosted the Montreal Canadiens before traveling to St. Louis for a Central Division rivalry game against the Blues. Chicago was finishing its pre-holiday slate with a back-to-back, which isn't easy in the middle of the long regular season.

The Friday night game against Montreal was the first time Bedard would face the Habs in Chicago. Having one of the big-market Canadian teams in town meant more media coming from north of the border. And, again, more eyeballs on Bedard's play.

The United Center was sold out and loud. Chicago anthem singer Jim Cornelison sang the Canadian anthem in French with Montreal in town before the crowd roared through "The Star-Spangled Banner." It was as loud of a crowd as the Blackhawks had played in front of since their home opener—it might have been louder.

Bedard was able to get the scoring started against the Canadiens, making a nice play to settle down a bouncing puck and set up Ryan Donato for the game's first goal. The Blackhawks would take a two-goal lead less than four minutes into the second period, but then they fell apart. The inconsistent effort and mistakes showed up again, and the Canadiens cashed in. Montreal scored five unanswered goals and the United Center faithful that had been so excited to start the game left quietly.

In the hallway outside the respective dressing rooms, it was obvious which team won the game. Mariah Carey's "All I Want for Christmas Is You" blasted out of the Montreal dressing room as the Habs celebrated a big comeback win in their final game before the break. When the media entered the Blackhawks' dressing room, a somber Jason Dickinson was waiting to discuss another implosion.

"They pushed and we didn't," the veteran center said. "It's really frustrating. Intentions are there, we want to do the right things. We want to win. We want to battle. But the execution isn't there all the time. It comes with being a young team, but at a certain point you just have to figure it out. It's as simple as that. You either figure it out or you don't, and time will tell whether what we're doing here is working."

The frustration was visible in his eyes and words. Before the door even opened, all the team's equipment was on its way to a truck to meet the players at the airport for St. Louis. The good—or bad—news after such a frustrating loss was the Blackhawks had one more chance at course correction before the Christmas break.

The following night, the disappointed Blackhawks were in St. Louis to face the Blues. And Wayne Gretzky, the greatest to ever lace up skates in the NHL, was in the house to watch the game.

The Blues scored the first goal of the night just three minutes into the game. But 45 seconds later, Bedard scored what was easily the front-runner for the NHL's goal of the season. He perfectly executed a "Michigan" goal—a lacrosse-style goal in which he picked the puck up on his stick blade and flipped it over Blues netminder Jordan Binnington's left shoulder into the net.

Bedard left the scene of the crime with his arms raised to the crowd as if to ask those in St. Louis, "Are you not entertained?" In his first trip to St. Louis to experience one of the terrific rivalries in the NHL, Bedard's first act was a memorable one.

During the intermission, Bedard was interviewed by Darren Pang on the Blackhawks' home broadcast. He nonchalantly explained, "There was just no one there. Just thought it was a good play, and yeah, kinda went for it."

"He's been fun to watch, and he's been better than we probably anticipated. Not only an ambassador on the ice, he's been tremendous off the ice for an 18-year-old man," Gretzky said on the Blues broadcast. "I'm happy for him. He's got the right coach in Luke Richardson, the right organization. But I couldn't do what he did tonight. That just wasn't in my repertoire. Hullie [Brett Hull] could do it. I could never do what [Bedard] did tonight. My daughter Emma is with me, and she goes, 'Dad, did you ever do that?' I said, 'No, I could never do that.'"

The goal had social media buzzing for the next few hours, and the Blackhawks offense followed Bedard's lead. When Nick Foligno scored a shorthanded goal at 5:16 into the third period, Chicago had a 5–2 lead.

And then it was déjà vu all over again. For a second consecutive night, the Blackhawks allowed five unanswered goals—this time all in the third period—and suffered another stunning collapse. This time, the final score was 7–5 and the Blackhawks were headed to a three-day break with two awful losses to think about until they returned to face the Winnipeg Jets on the 27th of December.

After the game, even after the Blackhawks gave up five unanswered goals for the second straight night, the questions were still about Bedard's goal.

"It was elite," Blues coach Drew Bannister said. "I don't know if you can defend that. It happens so quick, and it was clean. Binner, he didn't have a chance. I thought we could've been quicker to close when he was behind the net. That might've stopped that from happening. But that's a really highly skilled play by a good player."

The play was highlighted among the Top 10 plays of the night on ESPN's *SportsCenter*. It was No. 2 on a Saturday that was filled with college football bowl games and college and pro basketball. Bedard's name and "the Michigan" were trending on X (formerly Twitter) well into Sunday morning, and fans were still talking about it when they woke up the next day.

But the Blackhawks' defensive struggles were starting to rightfully steal headlines from the production of their star rookie. The team needed some time to regroup, try to get healthy, and sort out their issues.

The break came at a time when Bedard's offense was hot, however. His goal in St. Louis was only his third in the month of December and snapped a four-game drought for him in the scoring column, but he'd had five assists in his previous three games.

Heading into the Christmas holiday break, Bedard had scored 13 goals with 17 assists in 33 games. His 13 goals led all rookies in the NHL, two more than Minnesota center Marco Rossi. His 17 assists also led all rookies, one more than Anaheim defenseman Pavel Mintyukov. His 30 points were nine more than Rossi, who ranked second. And Bedard's 19:31 average ice time per night was almost 90 seconds per game more than any other rookie forward; the No. 2 overall pick from the summer's draft, Anaheim's Leo Carlsson, ranked second (in 10 fewer games).

According to official NHL statistics, only seven 18-year-old rookies in league history reached 30 points in fewer games than Bedard, and the names on the list are impressive: Ron

Francis (23), Dale Hawerchuk (27), Ryan Nugent-Hopkins (28), Sidney Crosby and Dan Quinn (29), Steve Yzerman (30), and Sylvain Turgeon (32). Alexandre Daigle also reached 30 points in 33 games.

The first 33 games of Bedard's NHL career had been both a highlight reel and a roller coaster of emotions. And he had only three more games after the holiday break to close out the most important calendar year of his life…so far.

CHAPTER 7

AN INVITE DEFERRED

T HE BLACKHAWKS' END to the pre-Christmas portion of the season came to a loud, resounding thud. And then they hit the road—literally. Because of weather in Chicago, the Blackhawks' travel party had to take buses back to Chicago from St. Louis following the painful loss in which they gave up five unanswered goals. After physical games on back-to-back nights, the Blackhawks had roughly 300 miles of road to think about the losses before having three days off.

Chicago was also set to hit the road when the games got started again after the break. After hosting the hot Winnipeg Jets on the first night back on the ice, the Blackhawks would play their next five games away from the United Center on a nine-day swing that started with two games in three nights in Dallas before the calendar flipped over to 2024.

The first time the Blackhawks could practice together after the three days away was the morning skate before hosting the Jets. Chicago was starting to get some of their injured players back into the lineup; forward Tyler Johnson missed the game in St. Louis but was able to return, as was defenseman Alex Vlasic. Most of the questions fielded by

Bedard after the morning skate weren't about what he got from Santa or players returning to the lineup. They were about his remarkable play in the Blackhawks' last game before the break.

Even with three days off for the entire NHL and the World Junior Championship getting started in Sweden on December 26, the buzz around the hockey world was still Bedard pulling off "the Michigan" in St. Louis—and Anaheim's Trevor Zegras doing it a couple hours later against Seattle.

Bedard got a text message from Zegras talking about them both scoring in the unique way on the same night, a rare accomplishment in the league. He said he thought Zegras' goal was "better" than his, saying, "He picked it up kind of with his toe there, so I think that's a little harder." Bedard also said it was "cool" to hear Wayne Gretzky was talking about his game that night in St. Louis.

But the Blackhawks and Bedard needed to leave that great individual play and the loss in St. Louis in the past and turn their attention to a tough slate coming up, starting with perhaps the best team in the Central Division at the time from Winnipeg.

The good news for Chicago: the Jets couldn't practice or travel before the day of the game either because of the Collective Bargaining Agreement, so they had to leave Winnipeg at 5:15 AM and fly into Chicago the morning of a game that started later than usual (it was an 8:00 PM local start in Chicago).

Hoping for a good start after their two losses before Christmas, the Blackhawks did the exact opposite; they weren't credited with a shot on goal for nearly 15 minutes to start the game. Bedard's line with Nick Foligno and Philipp Kurashev started generating some offense and got the Blackhawks on the board first. Bedard scored his first goal at the United Center since November 4, and it was a relentless, gritty goal that saw him crashing to the ice toward the goal post. The goal was his 12th score in a first period to date in the season, which led the entire NHL. It also extended Bedard's personal point streak to five games.

He wasn't done, though. And that streak of not scoring at home since the first game of November? A distant memory. Bedard ripped home the game-winning goal in overtime to win a dramatic game 2–1 in front of a packed United Center. During his interview on the bench after being named the game's First Star, he said, "It feels like home now. I'm super grateful to be here and to be a Blackhawk." And the adoring fans showed him all the love they could after a hard-fought victory.

The game-winner was his first in overtime and second game-winning goal of his career; his first came back on November 9 in Tampa during his memorable first two-goal, four-point night. And at 18 years, 163 days old, Bedard became the third-youngest player in NHL history to score a regular season overtime game-winning goal. Only Sidney Crosby and Jordan Staal did it at a younger age.

Bedard's family was in town for the holidays, and they were at the United Center for the first time since the Blackhawks' home opener. So they were able to see the incredible performance in person, which was special for Connor.

"Ever since I got drafted, there's been so much support. For myself and my family, we've said how good the people are [in Chicago], how welcoming it's been so far. To see that and to see just the support that we get every night, like I was saying, you can't help but love that and love the fans."

"It's always nice when they can be here and get to watch games," Bedard continued. "Obviously it's kind of nice to have a moment like that with them in the building. They're my biggest fans and they get pretty excited. It's cool that they've gotten to be there for a lot of my milestones—my first goal, first goal at home, and obviously first overtime goal. Little things like that, it's pretty cool.

"I give them more credit than I do myself for being here. They've done so much for me. To be able to enjoy some little things like that with them is pretty cool."

When asked by visiting media in Chicago about the atmosphere, Bedard frequently mentioned that the performance of "The Star-Spangled Banner" "never gets old" and that it gives him chills every game. Chicago's unique tradition of cheering through Jim Cornelison's performance (and Wayne Messmer's before him) dates back to the early 1980s. That aspect of the excitement in the United Center hadn't faded much in recent years as the team struggled, but there was a noticeable increase in the volume in the building after Bedard arrived.

He was becoming must-see TV and making Blackhawks home games the place to be in Chicago once again—just as Jonathan Toews and Patrick Kane had done nearly two decades earlier.

Following practice the day after his dramatic overtime game-winner, Bedard was asked about the roar in the United Center when he scored and if he ever dreams about how loud it could be for a playoff win.

"It's been unbelievable every game," Bedard said. "The support that we get is pretty special. Of course, watching some of the games in the finals of the past and everything, you're looking at the banners and stuff and thinking of that for sure. It's a special city to be playing sport. The fans are unreal. Can't imagine a better place to be playing.

"Obviously they're very passionate fans and the emotion. Yeah, that's pretty special to see people get so emotional and happy for us. We're going out there getting energy from them and playing for them. It's pretty special to see the emotion."

The next two Blackhawks games in Dallas could not have played out differently, especially for Bedard.

On December 29, the Blackhawks once again played a top team in their division into overtime. Chicago lost the game 5–4 in the closing seconds of the overtime with Dallas center Roope Hintz finishing off a hat trick performance. On the game-winning scoring play, which happened inside the final 10 seconds of OT, Bedard reached for a puck at the blue line for a potential breakaway. He didn't get the puck and Dallas converted a 3-on-2 to win the game.

Bedard finished the game with three shots on net but won only two of 13 faceoffs and was minus-three in the game.

Two nights later, on New Year's Eve, the Blackhawks found themselves on the wrong end of an 8–1 blowout loss. Bedard had an assist on Chicago's only goal, but was minus-three again and won only one of five faceoffs. During the game, Blackhawks head coach Luke Richardson once again had coaching moments with his young phenom.

"[Dallas'] second goal, it started in the O-zone. We talked about it; we have to be on top of them, and that was Connor going behind the net when he's got to be on top of his D in front of the net, who ended up scoring a goal," Richardson said after the game. "I think he wants to get it back right away and he's used to doing that, but I brought him in after the first period [and told him], 'You can't get everything back in one shift. You've just got to get back to playing on top of them and trusting your other players to turn pucks over. You're going to get chances.' Like the one he hit the post on in the first period. Instead of, we can't go rogue on our own and try to beat everybody up the ice. [Bedard doing that before Dallas' third goal] got everybody else off, and we're in scramble mode at that point in our D-zone. This team is too good for that. Dallas, they just feed off that."

Those conversations were ongoing with Bedard as he continued to learn the NHL game, even while the Blackhawks were seemingly losing players to injury every night. Chicago lost Taylor Raddysh during the first game in Dallas and Tyler Johnson during the second. But the relationship between Bedard and his head coach continued to be one that nurtured the young player. And Bedard appreciated his head coach being a positive influence on the room, even through some tough losses.

"If you just look at [Richardson], he's maybe a little intimidating," Bedard told Mark Lazerus of The Athletic during the trip. "But he's a super nice guy and easy to talk to. You always feel comfortable, you're never really nervous. You never want to make a mistake, but you're going to, and he's not going to be too harsh with you when you do."

Even with one point and a minus-six rating in his final two games of the 2023 calendar year, Bedard was named the NHL's Rookie of the Month for December, the second consecutive month he earned the recognition. He became the first player since St. Louis netminder Jordan Binnington in February and March of 2019 to win the award in back-to-back months. Bedard finished the month with five goals and 10 assists in 15 games.

After the lopsided loss in Dallas, the Blackhawks didn't take much time to lick their wounds. They needed to call up another body to fill out the roster for their next game in Nashville and had a hard, physical practice filled with battle drills on New Year's Day. The timing of the Blackhawks' five-game trip was becoming further complicated by the injuries that had plagued the team all year.

When the Blackhawks arrived at Bridgestone Arena in Nashville for their morning skate on January 2, there was a different vibe in the room—and it didn't relate to the injuries on the roster or the ugly loss in Dallas. Goaltender Petr Mrázek, who is from Czechia, was collecting on a few wagers in the room. His home country had upset Canada at the World Junior Championship that morning, which left Bedard and Korchinski feeling down for a group that could have been their teammates in the tournaments, and a few good friends.

"I know a lot of guys on the team, and being a Canadian, we take a lot of pride in that," Bedard said. "I just feel bad for those guys and how hard they played. It sucks, for sure."

Bedard did accept the playful, friendly roasting from Mrázek, saying he probably would have done the same if Canada had won the game. But it was clear the young Canadian, who had broken records in the previous edition of the World Juniors, was bummed because his friends had lost.

When the NHL game began that night, the Blackhawks had forward lines that weren't nearly as familiar as they would want in the middle of the regular season. And the task got tougher when Anthony Beauvillier, who started the game on a line with Bedard, left the game with a wrist injury during the second period.

Chicago was running out of healthy bodies up front at a rate that was almost comical at times, which made Bedard an even bigger focal point for opposing defenses. During the game in Nashville, Bedard's line—well, what was left of it— struggled to generate scoring chances in a 3–0 shutout loss. For the first time since the Blackhawks had hosted the Bruins on October 24, Bedard was held without a shot on goal.

With the mixing and matching continuing and the Blackhawks' roster in flux, another significant date on the calendar was approaching. On January 4, not only would Bedard play his first game at Madison Square Garden against the Rangers, but the National Hockey League would announce each team's representatives for the 2024 All-Star Game in Toronto.

Even if everyone were healthy, there was little question who Chicago's All-Star Game representative would be. Bedard led the team in goals, assists, points, and shots on goal. To be named an NHL All-Star in his rookie season was still an honor he didn't take lightly. And because of the NHL's obligation with Disney/ESPN, the Western Conference All-Stars were officially announced after the first intermission of the Penguins–Bruins game that overlapped with the Blackhawks at Rangers. But head coach Luke Richardson shared the news with Bedard earlier in the day.

At 18 years, 171 days old, Bedard became the youngest player ever named to an NHL All-Star Game. At just 18 years, 201 days, on February 3, 2024, Bedard could become the youngest player in NHL history to play for an NHL All-Star team. He could be the second youngest ever to play in the event, behind Toronto's Fleming MacKell (18 years, 166 days), who skated with the reigning Stanley Cup champion Maple Leafs at the inaugural showcase in 1947. Back in 1947, the All-Star Charity Game showcased the defending champions against a team of NHL All-Stars, so MacKell participated by virtue of being on the Leafs' roster at the time.

"I'm happy with being announced," Bedard said of his All-Star selection. "With our group, it has been a little frustrating lately with the results of the games. But it's good to get to go there and meet some of those guys. It should be fun."

"It's exciting. It's something you watch growing up. Seeing the list of guys going, it should be fun. I don't think about being the youngest too much; it's just exciting to be a part of it. I don't know if I would put it as a goal, but if you would have asked me if I wanted that, of course I would say 'Yes.' It's really exciting now that I get to go. I wasn't thinking about it too much. I was just going out there trying to play my best and if it happened, it happened. I'm grateful it did."

"When you can be with those guys, see how they act, how they are with people, it's definitely big and a bonus for me. Watching them and being around guys that have done everything in the league, it's good for me to learn from that."

The other nice part of Bedard being named an All-Star (that he didn't mention to the media)? He earned a $250,000 Type "A" performance bonus on his entry-level contract.

With the knowledge that he was an NHL All-Star in the back of his mind but also coming off a rare game in which he hadn't put a shot on net, Bedard also had the opportunity to do some impressive things in the so-called World's Most Famous Arena—Madison Square Garden in New York City.

The first period against the Rangers saw both sides of the young forward's game. He got pushed off the puck for a turnover by Vincent Trocheck that started the Rangers' first scoring play of the night. But later, inside the final minute of the first period, Bedard created a takeaway of his own and fed Ryan Donato for a good scoring chance.

Chicago hung around against arguably the best team in the Eastern Conference at the time, trailing only 2–1 heading to the third period. But the Rangers' depth took over and the home team skated away with a 4–1 victory.

For his first appearance at Madison Square Garden, Bedard put three shots on net and was minus-two. He failed to register a point for a third time in four games to begin the Blackhawks' road trip. The Blackhawks would stay in the New York area to play what looked like an exciting matchup the following night across the river against the New Jersey Devils.

When the Devils were in Chicago in early November, Jack Hughes and Nico Hischier—the Devils' two former No. 1 overall picks—were both out of the New Jersey lineup because of injuries. Since then, both had returned, and the Devils were fighting an uphill climb to get back into the playoff picture. The Blackhawks, meanwhile, where just trying to finish every game with the players who started it healthy.

The game in New Jersey started off physically, with the Devils and Blackhawks trading penalties in the first half of the opening period. When Devils defenseman Kevin Bahl went to the box to give Chicago their first power play, the Hawks hoped to take advantage.

As the Blackhawks generally do, the puck was dropped to Bedard to enter the offensive zone. As he crossed the blue line, the puck bounced a little and Bedard fumbled it a bit. Unfortunately, Devils forward/defenseman Brendan Smith—who is known to be a big hitter who occasionally crosses the line—was waiting for the Blackhawks' star like a brick wall.

Boom.

Bedard collided with Smith and went down in a heap. When he got back to his feet, Bedard immediately skated toward the Blackhawks' bench holding his mouth area while all hell broke loose on the ice. Nick Foligno and Philipp Kurashev went after Smith; no penalty was called for the hit on Bedard, but there were a few after the fact.

The tensions in the game continued to increase as big hits were dished out by both teams, many illegally. Bedard did not return. Foligno and Smith eventually dropped the gloves and fought in the second period, and Foligno did not return after they exchanged pleasantries. After the game on MSG—the Devils' television network—Smith said Foligno approached him about fighting before a faceoff and he accepted out of respect for the Blackhawks' veteran leader.

Jason Dickinson scored a power play goal in the first period, and Boris Katchouk scored a short-handed goal late in the second. The Blackhawks took a 2–1 lead into the third period, but without Bedard or Foligno for most of the game, Chicago once again just tried to hang around long enough to have a chance. The speed and skill of the Devils were too much to overcome, and Chicago lost another game, this time 4–2. Bedard departed after only skating 3:05 and with his status for the coming schedule unknown—just one day after learning he was an All-Star.

After the game, Blackhawks head coach Luke Richardson would only provide a minimal update on his team's superstar. "I haven't heard anything other than that everybody is coming home tonight—everybody is fine to come home…. There's nothing much we can do other than get them home, get them to our specialists, and see if everything is okay."

Dickinson said he spoke with Bedard between periods when he learned his night was over. "Connor was just really upset last night," Dickinson said. "That's pretty much all I talked to him about was just staying positive and being OK with where he's at."

"It's awful. I feel so bad for him," Dickinson continued. "He's having such a good year and he's such a good kid. He loves the game so much. I don't know what the timetable is, but to be out for any stretch of time, it just really sucks."

The Blackhawks flew back to Chicago after a winless five-game road trip on which they were outscored 24–8. Dickinson said the flight home was almost surreal. The players couldn't help but laugh at their awful fortune with five players—Bedard, Foligno, Anthony Beauvillier, Tyler Johnson, and Taylor Raddysh—all landing on IR during the five-game trip.

Meanwhile, Melanie Bedard, Connor's mother, boarded the first flight she could get to Chicago. She knew her son was hurt.

The team returned to the practice rink Saturday concerned for their young teammate—and Foligno—but also wondering who would be available to play on Sunday. The Blackhawks placed both Bedard and Foligno on IR on Saturday morning, confirming that Bedard had a fractured jaw. Foligno had fractured a finger in the fight with Smith that was a result of the big hit; Foligno was letting the Devils and other teams know that the Blackhawks wouldn't stand for teams taking shots at their star player.

A broken or fractured jaw injury usually has a return timetable of between four and seven weeks, which put Bedard's All-Star Game appearance in serious jeopardy; even Richardson acknowledged after the Saturday skate that it wasn't likely Bedard could participate in the events the first weekend in February, but he hoped his young star could still attend and be part of the atmosphere.

"I'm assuming they'd probably have him there," Richardson said. "He might not be able to participate, but it'd be good for him to get to go to that. It'd be a great honor to be there and follow through with what he's earned so far this year, and I'm sure the league would like that as well."

Richardson had suffered a broken jaw during his playing career (with Columbus in 2006), so he knew what it was like to deal with that injury. While the medical approach to the healing process had evolved since Richardson suffered the injury, the hard reality was not being able to be on the ice.

Before the Blackhawks' next game on Sunday afternoon against the Calgary Flames, Richardson said the team still didn't have a timeline for Bedard's potential return. The head coach said there was still some swelling in the area and the doctors wanted it to settle down before they could make a better assessment of the extent of the injury.

With all the injured players missing from the lineup, the Blackhawks were now in a unique, bad position. Chicago had more salary cap money on injured reserve than it had available to play in the game against Calgary. In fact, the 11 forwards the Blackhawks dressed against Calgary had a combined salary cap hit of only $13.9 million; they had approximately $24.9 million of just forwards on injured reserve.

"I don't think you replace those guys because of the talent level they have and leadership," veteran defenseman Connor Murphy said. "But still, each guy has to play their game. No one's going to be able to step out and play like Connor Bedard. Everyone has to play to their strengths and how they can and realize that, if everyone plays to their best ability and their own way, you're still going to have a chance to win."

The Blackhawks did just that, beating the Flames 4–3 with their depleted lineup. After the game, the players who spoke with the media talked about a bunker mentality and continuing to focus on a next-man-up approach to every game. Chicago added two forwards on Saturday out of necessity—Rem Pitlick via trade from Pittsburgh and Zach Sanford off waivers from Arizona—just to have enough bodies to play. Because of weather issues, Pitlick wasn't able to get to Chicago in time for the game against the Flames, but Sanford played despite not even having a single practice with his new team under his belt. And he acknowledged after the game that the injuries plaguing the Blackhawks were unlike anything he had seen.

"You ask anyone around the league, and they've never really seen anything like what's been going on with the Hawks here," Sanford said. "But for me, it's exciting, it's fun. It's a great organization to come into, a great city and great opportunity. So I'm just trying to make the most of it and have fun and then try to help the team win."

The schedule wasn't getting easier for the team without Bedard. Sadly, the one chance Blackhawks fans had to see him face Connor McDavid in Chicago during his first season came on a snowy Tuesday night on January 9. Without their electrifying rookie, the Blackhawks fought valiantly but came up short in a 2–1 loss. Chicago limited Edmonton to a season-low 15 shots on net, but McDavid scored the game-winning goal in highlight-reel fashion in the second period.

After the game, McDavid—who missed a significant part of his rookie season because of an injury—was asked about Bedard being out with an injury.

"It sucks," McDavid said. "I've been in his shoes before. There's no other way to say it other than it's a bad feeling. But things pass. He'll get healthy. He'll play at the top of his level again this year. Just stick with it and be positive and be a good teammate and enjoy the recovery process because it can be fun, and it can be exciting to get healthy again."

The following morning, the Blackhawks announced Bedard had had successful surgery on his jaw. The team expected him to miss six to eight weeks of action to recover from the injury, which meant his participation in the 2024 NHL All-Star Game was not going to happen.

Bedard lived in the same building as both his head coach and teammate Taylor Raddysh. Raddysh and his wife, also named Taylor, and their dog spent the night with Bedard to keep him company during a frustrating, scary time for the teenager. Bedard and Raddysh were developing a close relationship off the ice; the veteran was becoming a mentor for his young teammate, helping him adjust to the pro life and helping him compartmentalize the on-ice highs and lows and the demands away from the game.

The Blackhawks worked with chef Dee Dee Saracco to develop a food program for Bedard during his rehab. In fact, with Bedard living in the same building as Richardson, Saracco got some help delivering Bedard's first batch of food from the head coach when she arrived at the building in Chicago.

"I ran into her in our building and helped her unload her truck," Richardson said with a chuckle. "You know, like one of those hotel carts? It was full. So he's got lots of help."

Saracco, who had worked with the Blackhawks for five seasons, had previous experience creating meal plans for a player with a broken jaw. Defenseman Jarred Tinordi had shattered his jaw during the previous season, an injury that was worse than Bedard's injury. Tinordi is also a much bigger player than Bedard; he's listed as being eight inches taller.

Tinordi lost a lot of weight quickly after his injury, which was a concern initially with Bedard. Saracco worked closely with Jennifer Gibson, the Blackhawks' head of performance nutrition, to develop a program that included proteins and vitamins to help with his healing process and help him keep weight on as he began working to keep his body in shape to return. Prebiotics, probiotics, and collagen in shake form were the early diet.

Over time, Bedard graduated from that to lasagna (with a lot of cheese and some ground-up meat), meatloaf, mashed potatoes, sweet potatoes, and butternut squash. Those and some chicken, with the mix of supplements, went into the blender with some bone broth and it was a bit of a more robust shake.

Before the Blackhawks' game against the Dallas Stars on January 13, Nick Foligno met with the media. The team announced the day before that he had signed a two-year extension to stay with the team beyond his first season, a move that signaled some continuity in leadership for a team that was likely to get younger over the coming seasons. Foligno had been a strong voice in the room and an immediate friend of Bedard's. With this being the first time Foligno had spoken with the media since he'd fractured his finger fighting the player who injured Bedard, he was asked about how hard it was going to be to keep the teenager off the ice.

"Oh yeah. He's dying," Foligno said with a laugh. "It's pretty funny. The trainers were like, 'Hey, you kind of got to help us, he's not going to listen to us, so you've got to help us keep him at bay here a little bit,' so it's been pretty funny. He's like, 'I feel fine,' I'm like, 'Man, just pump the brakes a little bit.' But that's who he is. That's why you love him, and I'm sure he'll come back an even better version of himself, which is a scary thought."

The Blackhawks lost the game to Dallas later that night in another hard-fought effort with limited offense. Bedard's teammates were hanging in games with some of the better teams in the NHL but simply didn't have enough offensive firepower to finish games with a win. Richardson gave his team Sunday off after the Dallas game not only to recover but also to stay out of the terrible weather in Chicago. Between blizzard conditions and plummeting temperatures, the fact the Blackhawks had almost 19,000 fans at the game against Dallas spoke to how much fans were embracing the team, even with Bedard out of the lineup. But they needed a day off before playing three games in four nights—with travel to and from Buffalo in the middle.

On that Monday, days after Bedard had surgery to repair his jaw, the Blackhawks had practice on Martin Luther King

Jr. Day in Chicago. Schools were off for the holiday, but the weather in Chicago was cold. The wind chills reported around the area were negative 15 to negative 20 degrees Fahrenheit, with overnight lows dipping into the negative 10–15 degree range without the wind. A lot of people around Chicago were understandably staying home and indoors. But fans still showed up to see the Blackhawks—without Bedard—practice on the holiday.

When the players and media entered the dressing room after practice, everyone was surprised to see Bedard in full gear and a green, no-contact jersey ready to rejoin his teammates on the ice. He had a full bubble attached to his helmet like he had worn for Canada in tournaments previously. Just one week removed from facial surgery, Bedard was getting back on the ice to start skating already.

Kevin Korchinski said he was surprised to see him out there, but head coach Luke Richardson could only joke about keeping the rink rat away from the ice.

"Really? He's out there?" Richardson laughed with a sly smile when speaking with the media after that Monday practice. "He's been begging, and I think they said it's okay. But he's been given specific instructions: he's not allowed to take slap shots, he's not allowed to really clench. So if they see that, they might pull the rug out from under him. I think he's just eager and it will be good for him to get moving. He just has to be very careful, like early stages of clenching. I don't know if he can even put anything in there because he's still got—not completely wired shut—but I think it's elastic bands on it that keep it so that there's a minimal amount of movement."

Richardson did say that, even though he was already skating, Bedard's appearance on the ice did not have any impact
on the six-to-eight-week timeline the team had given for his
recovery. He was just going to work on the things he could,
as allowed by the doctors, while allowing his jaw time to fully
heal. Still, seeing Bedard on the ice that quickly after his surgery was a positive for his teammates and the fans who stayed
around to watch practice.

Before the Blackhawks hosted the San Jose Sharks—a battle
of the teams with the two worst records in the NHL at the
time—on a frigid Tuesday, January 16, Bedard was on the
ice again with prospect Sam Savoie, who had suffered a broken femur during a preseason game, and Foligno. This time,
Bedard was wearing a black jersey, taking shots on the United
Center ice before the rest of the Blackhawks took the ice for
their morning skate. As Foligno and Savoie left the ice, Bedard
made sure to sprint a few extra laps as the Zamboni was
starting to clean off the ice. A race to get in more work as
the Zamboni was on the ice was a sign of things to come in
Bedard's recovery.

Without Bedard available, the Blackhawks offense continued to struggle. They were able to beat the Sharks, who had
the worst record in the league at the time, but they needed
an extended, nine-round shootout to get the second point
in the standings. Then the Blackhawks flew to Buffalo for
what was supposed to be a game on that Wednesday night.
The weather in Buffalo was so bad the city was shut down by
local government. The Blackhawks were able to get into their
hotel, but the game was pushed back a day for safety. The
Blackhawks got shut out before coming home and hosting

the New York Islanders in their final game before the All-Star break.

The Islanders arrived in Chicago struggling in their own right. This game needed overtime, just like the game against San Jose earlier in the week. The Hawks were able to win this one in overtime before a shootout. The day after the game, the Islanders announced the firing of their head coach, Lane Lambert. Hall of Fame goaltender Patrick Roy took over at the helm for the Isles. And social media made jokes at the Blackhawks' expense, saying a loss to the lowly Blackhawks was bad enough that it got a coach fired.

After the Islanders game, the Blackhawks embarked on a four-game road trip to western Canada and Seattle. Bedard continued skating on his own in Chicago, but this was a tough trip for him to miss. Monday, January 22, was supposed to be the first time Bedard played against his hometown Canucks in Vancouver. Richardson and Foligno mentioned it was hard on the teenager to miss a trip that he had circled on the schedule from the moment he was drafted in June.

While Bedard continued to skate to keep in shape and be ready for the moment his jaw was healed enough to return to practices and game action, the Blackhawks were swept on the four-game trip. In the four games in Vancouver, Seattle, Edmonton, and Calgary, the Hawks were outscored 12–2. It was becoming increasingly apparent that Chicago needed Bedard to drive its offense; even with all the other injuries suffered by veteran players throughout the season to date, the most noticeable impact on the offense was the removal of the rookie forward.

In the 11 games between Bedard's injury and the All-Star break, the Blackhawks' offense completely disappeared. Their scoring fell from averaging 2.31 goals per game to just 1.27—easily the worst in the entire NHL. The Blackhawks' power play fell by three full percentage points, from 13 to 10, without Bedard, and the team's overall shooting percentage dropped from 8.8 to 4.8. The statistical shift in the wake of one injury was undeniable, even for a first-year player.

When the NHL announced All-Star Game replacements for a couple injured players, including Bedard, the league did not extend an invitation to another member of the Blackhawks. For the first time in 20 years, there would not be a Chicago Blackhawk participating in the All-Star Game.

Fans were sad that the opportunity to see Bedard compete against the likes of Connor McDavid, Auston Matthews, Nathan MacKinnon, and others in the skills competitions would not happen. But...

On the morning of February 2, the day of the NHL's skills competition, Bedard was indeed in Toronto. He received the IIHF's Male Player of the Year Award that morning in a ceremony at the Hockey Hall of Fame, his first social appearance since his jaw surgery that wasn't on the ice. He was around the other All-Stars, joking around and taking photos with the likes of Connor McDavid and Nathan MacKinnon, Mitchell Marner and Cale Makar.

Bedard looked happy to be in an environment he had dreamed of since he was a young kid. Even if he couldn't play in the game or compete in the skills competition, being around other hockey players was his happy place.

Later in the afternoon, when players arrived at Scotiabank Arena for the skills competition, Bedard walked in with MacKinnon. The Colorado Avalanche shared an image of the two on their social channels with the caption, "A couple #1 overall picks in the building." The Blackhawks shared images of Bedard sitting in front of his jersey with the All-Star Game patch on the shoulder. He was in attendance with the rest of the All-Stars.

When the skills competition began, that jersey that had been behind him in a locker in the room was now on his body. Bedard was in full Blackhawks gear and skates, and was introduced to the packed house in Toronto as one of the passers for the one-timer competition. The other passer: Sidney Crosby, the player Bedard had grown up idolizing like so many other young Canadian players.

Bedard, a right-handed shooter, was tasked with passing to the right-handed shooters. Crosby was passing to the left-handers. Bedard's pass recipients: Boston Bruins forward David Pastrňák, New York Islanders forward Mathew Barzal, and MacKinnon. MacKinnon won the event with 23 points.

Bedard briefly spoke with the NHL Network's Jamison Coyle and Tony Luftman at the arena before and after taking the ice for his passing moment.

"I feel good," he told Luftman with a smile after helping the shooters compete. "Obviously it's up to the docs now."

With Bedard making an appearance at the event, other stars were asked about him missing time because of the injury. A few of the players participating over the weekend had dealt with injuries during their own careers and could relate personally to what he was going through as a rookie. No All-Star put on a bigger show on that Friday night than the eventual skills competition champion, Edmonton's Connor McDavid. He too missed a significant portion of his rookie campaign because of injury.

"Obviously you feel for him," McDavid told NHL.com's Tracey Myers after the event. "You know, getting hurt [stinks] no matter who you are, especially someone that is so devoted to the game as he is. It's a bad break and I'm sure he's wishing he can be partaking in some of the events. It was great to see him on the ice looking healthy and looking like he is close to coming back. It was great to see him out there."

CHAPTER 8

41 DAYS

THE BLACKHAWKS RETURNED after their bye week and the All-Star break without Bedard available—still. But he was skating in a green jersey before their first practice on Monday, February 5, without the previous limitations on skating or shooting the puck hard. He looked like a player who was close to being back, and his work showed that he wanted to be ready for game action as soon as the doctors cleared him.

After that first practice, Bedard returned to the dressing room at Fifth Third Arena at the same time as Lukas Reichel, whose locker stall was right next to Bedard's. When the two sat down, the cameras from local television stations crowded around and writers approached. Reichel half-jokingly asked if the media was there for him or Bedard. It was for Reichel; media couldn't talk to players who were on the injured list. But the question received a good laugh from everyone in the room—including Bedard.

When he spoke with the media, head coach Luke Richardson had to reiterate that the timeline for Bedard to return had not changed, even if he'd looked healthy at the events in Toronto over the weekend. Richardson did say,

171

however, that the coaches were going to begin strategically tailoring their practice schedules so he could take part in some of the rushes with his teammates.

The next day, Bedard was out early again. But this time, he stayed on the bench with his teammates and did take part in some of the practice elements. Nick Foligno playfully hugged him into the boards and his teammates were all talking to him as he started skating with them. And, again, after practice he skated with skills coaches to get in extra work. It did not appear that Bedard had lost a step or weight while he had been out. And he was starting to get back to shooting the puck with the precision that had already become his trademark.

In the background, the Bedard Effect was living around the Blackhawks organization. NBC Sports Chicago, the team's local rightsholder, ranked second in the NHL in viewership increase over the previous season, reporting a 38 percent increase. That ranked behind only the Anaheim Ducks in the entire NHL.

On the morning of the second practice after the break, the *Chicago Sun-Times* broke the story that the Blackhawks would be awarded the 2025 Winter Classic. The team confirmed that the Blackhawks would host their rivals from St. Louis at Wrigley Field for the event. It was another seemingly full-circle moment for the Blackhawks, who hosted the Detroit Red Wings at Wrigley Field in the Winter Classic in 2009. The 2009 event was awarded before the Blackhawks had qualified for the playoffs with the roster that, for the most part, would eventually win the 2010 Stanley Cup. But, at that time, the Blackhawks were a non-factor on the international stage.

Going back to Wrigley Field against the Blues was a head-line-grabbing piece of news, and it all centered around how

The scene in Nashville when the Blackhawks made Bedard the first overall pick in the 2023 NHL Draft. (Luke Hales/Getty Images)

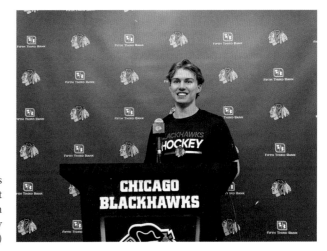

Bedard was all smiles when he arrived at training camp in September. (Photo by Tab Bamford)

During training camp, Bedard didn't have a locker stall yet—like the other rookies trying to make the team. (Photo by Tab Bamford)

Fans from all over North America and beyond traveled to see Bedard's rookie season. (Joel Auerbach/ Getty Images)

Bedard frequently spoke about how special it is to be part of "The Star-Spangled Banner" at the United Center. (Jamie Sabau/Getty Images)

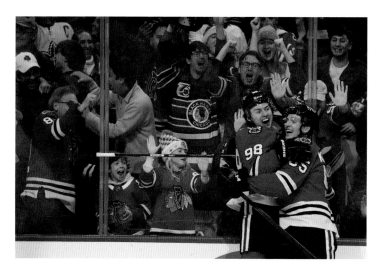

Bedard and Kevin Korchinski were two of the youngest players in the NHL during their rookie seasons. (Patrick McDermott/ Getty Images)

The No. 1 overall picks from the 2023 NHL and NBA Drafts—Bedard and Victor Wembanyama of the San Antonio Spurs—spent some time together in Chicago. (Chris Ramirez/ NHLI via Getty Images)

Connor vs. Connor—on December 12, Bedard scored a goal in his first matchup against McDavid in Edmonton. (Andy Devlin/NHLI via Getty Images)

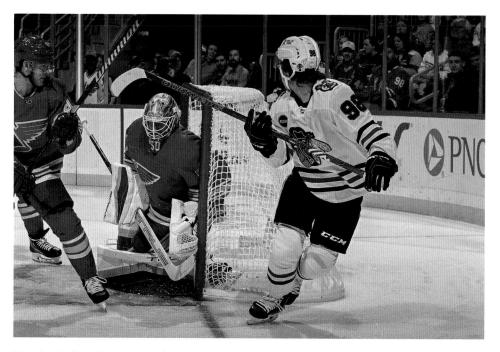

Two days before Christmas, Bedard scored a "Michigan" style goal in St. Louis. (Scott Rovak/NHLI via Getty Images)

Even though he couldn't play in the 2024 NHL All-Star Game, Bedard attended and spent time with other stars. (Mark Blinch/NHLI via Getty Images)

On behalf of the Blackhawks and NHL, Bedard announced the Winter Classic would return to Wrigley Field. (Chase Agnello-Dean/NHLI via Getty Images)

Media surrounds Bedard in the Blackhawks' dressing room following his first game back after his injury. (Photo by Tab Bamford)

For the final 29 games of Bedard's rookie season he took the ice with a bubble attached to his helmet to protect his broken jaw. (Bill Smith/NHLI via Getty Images)

Bedard had plenty to celebrate during a historic rookie season. (Chase Agnello-Dean/NHLI via Getty Images)

Bedard had changed the appeal of the Blackhawks. Chicago had played in a half-dozen outdoor games with the core of Toews, Kane, Keith, and Seabrook. But it had been six years since the Blackhawks had been asked to play in one of the league's signature events.

The Blackhawks were back as a national brand, and it was because of Bedard. After all, Bedard's regular season debut in Pittsburgh had drawn a bigger national television audience in the United States than the 2024 Winter Classic between the Seattle Kraken and Vegas Golden Knights.

Chicago's first game back from the break was against the Minnesota Wild. It was the second half of a nationally televised doubleheader on TNT. During the first intermission of the opening game of the night (between the Rangers and Lightning), the NHL made the announcement of the 2025 Winter Classic official via press release. To the national audience in the United States, the news was broken by Bedard himself—who was standing behind home plate at Wrigley Field live.

"On behalf of the Chicago Blackhawks, we're very excited to announce that we'll be hosting the 2025 NHL Winter Classic versus the St. Louis Blues here at Wrigley Field," Bedard told the cameras. "So we're all pretty pumped."

The panel, including former NHL players Chris Chelios, Anson Carter, and Paul Bissonnette with host Liam McHugh, then asked Bedard questions about adjusting to life in the NHL, his experience at the All-Star Game in Toronto, and finally, what it was like to be the 18-year-old face of the franchise announcing an NHL signature event on live television from historic Wrigley Field. As always, Bedard handled their questions easily.

The TNT crew did not ask Bedard specifically when he would return to the ice, but McHugh did mention the next time they would have the Blackhawks on their network was two weeks from that Wednesday night. The Blackhawks would host nine of their 10 games in February, which gave the team—and Bedard—plenty of practice time close to home to get bodies back into the lineup.

The Wild would come to Chicago featuring defenseman Brock Faber, who was emerging as a strong contender along with Bedard for the Calder Memorial Trophy.

Even though Bedard had missed almost the entire month of January, he was still the betting favorite to win the league's Rookie of the Year award. But Faber was on his heels, playing very well on a Minnesota team that was struggling with its own injuries. Still, national pundits continued to point to how much the Blackhawks offense had fallen off without Bedard in the lineup as adding to his perceived value, and keeping him the favorite to win the award despite missing so much time.

Chicago lost to the Wild that night 2–1. Faber factored in the game-winning goal with the second assist on Marcus Foligno's marker in the third period. The Blackhawks were credited with one (1) single shot on net in the first period, coming up just short of making Minnesota history; the Wild had never allowed zero shots on goal in a full period. The only shot on goal that counted for the Hawks was from 100 feet out from Nick Foligno, who scored their only goal of the night.

With each day of practice, Bedard was putting in an increasingly strenuous effort to ready himself for game action. But the doctors still needed to clear him for a return date, so wearing the same green non-contact jersey and full bubble on his bucket each day was his required wardrobe.

Two nights after losing to the Wild, the Blackhawks faced one of league's top teams, the New York Rangers. The Rangers were going through a bit of an identity crisis of their own, with some controversy surrounding the status of their goaltenders. Veteran Jonathan Quick had taken more starts than Igor Shesterkin in recent weeks, leading some to wonder if the two-time Stanley Cup champion from his days with the LA Kings was now the top netminder in New York. Shesterkin got the start in Chicago in his first attempt to show he was ready for the post-All-Star-break stretch run.

On this night, once again without Bedard available, the Hawks were able to take an early lead when Alex Vlasic found the back of the net only 2:39 into the first period. There was some optimism in a United Center that included a decent number of Rangers fans; the Original Six matchup usually saw plenty of blue shirts in the stands, and Rangers fans are vocal in their support.

The Rangers scored twice in the four minutes following Vlasic's goal and added a third goal in the second period to take what felt like an insurmountable 3–1 lead to the third period. Once again, the Blackhawks were struggling to generate any offense at all. But they got a spark when Nick Foligno scored at 13:37 into the third period. Inside the final two minutes, Jason Dickinson scored the Blackhawks' first goal with their goaltender on the bench for an extra attacker to tie the game. Regulation expired and the game moved on to an exciting overtime.

Unfortunately, a broken play turned into a goal for the Rangers and the Blackhawks lost for the sixth straight game. Afterward, Foligno talked about taking some positives away from a game in which the team skated with a very good

Rangers team and were able to get it to overtime. But he was also mindful that a loss is still a loss, and the NHL is a results-driven enterprise.

Chicago practiced on Saturday before having Sunday off to watch the Super Bowl. When they returned to the practice rink on Monday, head coach Luke Richardson gave the media the most positive update yet regarding the status of his young superstar. Bedard did not get his usual Monday imaging done this week because the doctors felt the previous week that he was progressing well on the timeline to return. This Monday was five weeks after his surgery, and Richardson said the team hoped to check in with the doctors late in the week to see how soon he could return. But the hope for all involved was that a good word from the doctor would make Bedard available at some point during the following week.

"I think they just thought everything was on course, so I think maybe later in the week or early next week is probably when they're targeting for hopefully the last one," Richardson said. "They just said it was useless to take another image with radiation. Everything was on pace and looks to be on the same timeline that they thought."

"Knowing him, he'll try to get back before, which would be great," Richardson continued. "But we're just going to leave it as is and in the doctor's hands until next Monday to kind of go from there."

With those details in mind, everyone started plotting the course for Bedard's timeline. Richardson was asked if Bedard would get his scan done in time to make the trip with the team to Carolina on the following Monday for the Blackhawks' only road game of the month of February, and he chuckled a bit.

"That's right on the deadline and I'm not sure if he's going to be able to get to a doctor on the six-week mark and get himself to Carolina," Richardson said with a wry smile. "He might, but I don't know if that'll happen."

The week following that positive update was one that Bedard undoubtedly had circled on his calendar since before his rookie season began nearly five months earlier. On Tuesday night, Bedard's hometown Vancouver Canucks visited the United Center for the second time of the season. When they met on December 17, Bedard was credited with five shots on net and had two assists in a 4–3 Blackhawks loss. The only trip the Blackhawks would make to Vancouver during the regular season was on January 22—without Bedard.

Two days after the Canucks visited the United Center, Sidney Crosby made his only trip to Chicago. The Pittsburgh Penguins were slated to play the second half of a back-to-back on Thursday night in Chicago. And two days later, the Blackhawks had a rare 2:00 PM local start against the Ottawa Senators.

Bedard's Monday practice had a lot of energy from a young player who wasn't likely to play for at least another week. He was ripping one-timers and skating with a game-day-like approach. He attended the morning skate on Tuesday before the Canucks game and got in extra work before again going through more game simulation drills with coaches before the rest of the team took the ice.

That game against the Canucks was one of the worst the Blackhawks had played during the season to that point. As they had against Minnesota the previous week, the Blackhawks put only one shot on net in the entire first period. This time, it was a weak one-timer from Seth Jones, who admitted after the game that the entire bench—like the fans—knew they were at zero and he felt they just needed to get one on the board before the intermission. Jones' shot came with 28 seconds left in the period and received a Bronx cheer from the United Center faithful.

As they had been against the Rangers, the Blackhawks found themselves down 3–1 heading to the third period. This time, their opponent added a fourth goal and didn't give the Hawks much of a chance to get back into the game. Kevin Korchinski scored his first goal since November 24 (his overtime game-winner against Toronto) late in the third period to make the final score 4–2.

After the game, Jones and Korchinski spoke with the media. They both stressed that their effort that night was unacceptable. After a strong performance, albeit in a losing effort, against the Rangers, they never showed up for a game against a Vancouver team that came in with the best record in the entire NHL.

Head coach Luke Richardson was about as frustrated as he had been in any postgame media session during his tenure as the head coach of the Blackhawks. The only player he singled out for performing well that night was goalie Petr Mrázek.

"I think we've been proud of how the guys have worked over the last month, but not tonight," Richardson said. "That wasn't the same effort. Kind of the same result in pulling the goalie and putting a little pressure on at the end, but not the way we want to do things around here. We started out OK the first part of the game and that was a good first penalty kill. But right after we killed that first penalty, it went downhill. They turned their speed up and their determination level and we didn't. We definitely didn't match it, nowhere even close. They really showed where they are in the standings and showed us where we are. So that's nothing to be proud of tonight, the way we played. Other than Petr."

Richardson went on to say he thought about giving the team Wednesday off because they had games every other day for nearly two straight weeks, but they would be back at Fifth Third Arena the following day to work on things that hadn't been good in the loss. And there were plenty of things to work on.

The Wednesday practice had plenty of energy, but it also had a few eyebrows raised once again. Young forward Lukas Reichel, who had been in and out of Richardson's doghouse throughout the season and had been struggling a great deal, was skating out of the rotation with Bedard and Rem Pitlick (who was placed on waivers after practice). It appeared Reichel, the team's first-round pick in 2020, was going to be a healthy scratch when a struggling Pittsburgh team arrived the next day.

Even though his coach had said just two days prior that the doctors didn't need to meet with Bedard until later in the week, the team set up an appointment in the morning and late on Wednesday afternoon to get another look at how he was healing and discuss how soon he could be back on the ice. Bedard wanted to be back as soon as possible—he wanted to face Sidney Crosby. But he hadn't taken any physical contact in almost six full weeks, so the doctors, coaches, and front office all needed to consider the long-term plan and keeping Bedard in the best place physically.

The doctors liked what they saw.

Bedard felt good.

There was a chance…

At 9:35 AM CT on the day of the Penguins game, Sportsnet's Elliotte Friedman posted on X, "Word this morning that Blackhawks and Connor Bedard are checking in with doctors about the possibility of playing tonight vs Pittsburgh. We will see what the day brings, but the good news is his return is close."

The hockey world's attention was secured. Was it really possible that, despite assurances from Richardson just three days earlier that Bedard wouldn't play until the following week, Bedard could actually suit up against Crosby and the Penguins?

Even though the team did not have a full team morning skate (which also meant no media eyes to watch), Bedard joined a few other injured players and scratches on the ice. The coaches, including Richardson, put him through some physical tests to see how he felt after getting hit a few times in game-like scenarios.

Bedard still felt good.

It was go time.

Other hockey insiders and media personalities started to chime in with reports that Bedard might play. But there was still no confirmation from any official sources saying he was cleared.

That was, until 1:45 PM CT, when the Blackhawks' official X account tweeted a highlight video of Bedard that simply read, "asked my boss and they said I could share this video today."

Social media was buzzing. Since his injury, fans had really only seen Bedard briefly on the ice at the All-Star Game in Toronto and then announcing the Winter Classic on TNT. Now, he was suddenly—surprisingly—returning to game action 41 days after breaking his jaw against the Devils. And of course, playing against Crosby was a big part of him wanting to return for this specific game.

"I'm sure [Bedard] was really excited at the beginning of the year and I know he spent some time with [Crosby] at the All-Star Game and the NHL event before the season," Richardson said before the game. "When competitors like that play against each other, they ramp up. They really respect each other, but when the game's on, that's another extra element. If you can win that game, it's a little bit of bragging rights maybe for the next event."

Richardson said he didn't expect Bedard to have any restrictions on time despite missing 14 games. And he was going to slot into the lineup between Nick Foligno and Philipp Kurashev, right where he left off before the injury.

How badly did the Blackhawks miss Bedard? The team scored only 20 goals in the 14 games he was out of the lineup. They were the only team in the entire NHL to average less than two goals per game over that 41-day span of time.

Bedard was in the starting lineup for the game, taking the opening faceoff against Crosby just as he had in his first career NHL game. Bedard lost the faceoff and then lost track of Crosby. Pittsburgh's captain scored 15 seconds into the game to give the Penguins a 1–0 lead.

Welcome back, Connor.

Later in the first period, Bedard tried a pass all the way across the blue line entering the offensive zone. It got picked off and went the other way, ending with Reilly Smith scoring Pittsburgh's second goal of the night.

Understandably, there was some rust to kick off in his first game action in six weeks. Bedard had been skating, shooting, and working hard, but that isn't navigating an NHL defense and making plays at game speed. The Blackhawks took a two-goal deficit to the room after a first period in which Bedard skated 4:48. His line did not have a single shot attempt in the first period—the only Chicago line of forwards that failed to even attempt to get the puck on net.

When the puck dropped to begin the second period, it quickly appeared that Bedard had successfully worked through the rust. He was popping passes through traffic, weaving through defenders, and creating chances for himself and his teammates. Eight minutes into the second period, Bedard received a nice pass from Nick Foligno, made a couple defenders miss, and drew enough attention to himself that Philipp Kurashev was wide open on the back door. Bedard found him, Kurashev scored, and the Blackhawks were within one.

The assist was the only point Bedard would produce in a 4–1 loss, but he and Kurashev quickly rediscovered the chemistry they had before the injury. Both players were flying and finding each other for chances. After failing to be on the ice for a shot attempt for the Blackhawks in the opening period, Bedard finished the night leading all Chicago forwards in that regard. He was on the ice for 19 Blackhawks shot attempts in 21:17—the most ice time of any Chicago forward in the game. He finished tied for the team lead with four shots on goal; was credited with two takeaways; and, yes, tied for the team lead with two hits.

Coming off a broken jaw that cost him 41 days of action, Bedard was willing to initiate contact without fear.

After the game, Bedard admitted to being antsy and excited to be back. "[I] felt like a kid," he joked after the game. And he acknowledged it took him a few shifts to get his legs under him in the first period. But after that, he was back doing what he loves to do: playing hockey.

The swarm of media around Bedard after the game was larger than many postgame scrums in recent weeks. This was the first time since his injury that Bedard had been made available to any media other than national broadcasts at the All-Star Game and for the announcement of the Winter Classic, so there were so many questions that hadn't been asked yet. And, after skating a heavy workload—especially in the third period—in his first game back, Bedard calmly answered every question with composure and ease. The first question everyone wanted to know but hadn't been able to ask was: Did he know he was hurt when he got hit? And did he know it was bad?

"It was just weird," he said. "My face was numb and stuff, and my bite was off, which was kind of the only thing. They told me that it was broken. I just thought of [Bruins defenseman Zdeno] Chára going back in the bubble, so I didn't think too much of it. But obviously it's not Game 7 of the Cup Final. You've got to wait and let it heal. It sucked, but right in the moment, I knew something was a little weird, but you never really know."

Bedard didn't want to say much about the conversation he had with the Blackhawks' front office about returning as early as he did, other than to say it was a collaborative decision. However, he did not shy away from saying he wanted to be back sooner. He understood the ultimate decision needed the approval of the doctors, coaches, and management, though, as well as him feeling confident that it was time.

"I've been skating for whatever, four weeks now," he said. "I felt confident coming in because of that, I think. But, also, you kind of feel normal and you're on the sidelines, so that sucks. But I was fortunate to be able to skate and work out the whole time, so I don't want to look at that as a negative.

"I'm not going to go in there scared. If it happens—I don't know, you just don't think about it, really. I'm confident in myself and my abilities. You can't be nervous going out there."

After Jarred Tinordi lost as much weight as he did with his broken jaw, the fact that Bedard looked good and was able to play as well and as much as he did in his first game back was a credit to his commitment to staying on program with his diet and nutrition. He cracked a big smile when he mentioned his mom being with him throughout his recovery to help him with food prep, and noted that Dee Dee Saracco had been a big help with him having the right food to eat.

Bedard had been able to transition to eating full meals—including chewing solid food—a couple weeks before his return. Managing what and how much he consumed every day while continuing to work hard on the ice made a significant contribution to his being able to return on the timeline that he did against Pittsburgh. The commitment to what needed to be done impressed his friend and the de facto captain of the team, Nick Foligno.

"I think he was a little confused," Foligno said about Bedard's reaction to the injury the night it happened. "Then, once he saw the pictures, he realized the difference. But give him tons of credit. He worked his butt off to get back. Every day, he was in here—too long, some days, for the trainers' liking. But that's how badly he wants it. He wants to be the best, and no setback is going to curb his ability to get better in certain facets. I was proud of him for that. He was really mature in how he handled a significant injury, especially early in his career."

Overall, it was an impressive return for a young star the league had centered so much of its attention on before his injury. As he continued to increase his work in practices, he also showed the coaches that he was physically ready. The confidence Richardson had expressed before the game when formally announcing that Bedard would indeed be back in the lineup appeared to be well placed. After the game, he was equally impressed with how his 18-year-old superstar had returned confidently.

"I thought he skated well, and I thought he had some pep in his stride," Richardson said. "He looked raring to go. They had a tough first shift and just a quick goal against…. As the game went on, they looked really good and, yeah, he looked confident on the power play. He looked confident out there, just like he always is, and made some really good plays."

In the other dressing room, Bedard's hero sat in his locker stall answering questions himself. Crosby scored twice that night, giving him 30 goals on the season. In doing so, Crosby established a new Penguins record by scoring 30 for the 12th consecutive season, moving past Mario Lemieux. That consistent production is a reason so many young hockey players in Canada admire Crosby. Even on a night when his team picked up a desperately needed win and he made franchise history, Crosby spoke about the young Blackhawk who some felt might be the next…well, Crosby.

"He looked pretty good for coming off an extended time being injured and getting back into it," Crosby said. "He's a special player and there are times when it doesn't look like he's got a lot of room and he's making something out of nothing."

He did look good, but the Blackhawks lost their eighth straight game. And they only scored one goal in yet another defeat. There was a tough reality continuing to evolve with the Blackhawks. The players were obviously frustrated with the results every night, and the coaches were pressing for improved play and wins. But there was also the underlying understanding that this team was missing some important players because of injuries, and young players were still learning and developing. Still, the struggle to stay upbeat in the face of so many losses was weighing on the players around Bedard in the room.

When the Blackhawks took the ice for their Friday practice before hosting Ottawa for a Saturday matinee game, they were greeted by a couple young skaters. Landon and Hudson Foligno were on the ice with their father, Nick, starting to dream about becoming third-generation NHL players. They skated around and took some shots before the rest of the Blackhawks were ready for practice to start and then were in the dressing room as the team departed the ice.

Richardson once again talked about how to balance the learning curve for some of his young players—the long game—with the immediate need for results in the NHL. He had a long conversation with Lukas Reichel near the end of practice about some specific elements of his game the coaches wanted him to work on before he could return to the lineup. Reichel was going to be a healthy scratch against the Senators the next day. Even though he brought a lot of offensive potential to a roster that, for the most part, lacked exactly that, the coaches were still working on the fine details of his game and needed to see more.

That level of accountability included Bedard. Richardson and Foligno both spoke regularly about how Bedard's defensive game was underrated but also pointed out that it continued to be a work in progress for him as well. In the game against Pittsburgh, Kurashev admitted that there was some confusion on his part because he had moved back to wing after playing center on Chicago's top line for most of Bedard's absence. With injuries forcing so many lineup changes, players needed to communicate better and more frequently than ever. Bedard needed some time to get himself back to game speed both physically and mentally in his first game back. By the end of the night, though, he and Kurashev had things figured out fairly well.

Chicago's next home game was a Saturday matinee against the Ottawa Senators. This would be the first time Bedard faced the team based in Canada's capital. The Senators came in having already made a coaching change during their season and struggling to find consistency, but certainly playing much better than the struggling Blackhawks.

Bedard started a scoring play that ended with Foligno tapping in a Kurashev pass in the first period to give the Blackhawks a 1–0 lead. As it had been throughout the season, Chicago failed to hold or extend its lead. Ottawa tied the game less than three minutes later and took a 2–1 lead early in the second period on a power play goal from Luke Richardson's nephew, Senators defenseman Jakob Chychrun.

During the season, the Blackhawks had been marketing their weekend games toward a younger crowd, calling them the "Best Day Ever." With in-house DJs, kids taking on roles in the in-game entertainment and announcing, and more kid-friendly action around the game, they had been a successful venture in getting lively crowds into the United Center. This Saturday afternoon was no different, even though the two teams on the ice were near the bottom of the NHL standings.

When Bedard tied the game at two with a fabulous goal less than three minutes after Ottawa had taken the lead, the crowd erupted. It was Bedard's first goal since returning from his injury and gave him his first multi-point game since he'd scored twice against the Winnipeg Jets two days after Christmas.

Bedard wasn't done. It appeared he scored a second goal to give the Blackhawks a 3–2 lead at 12:24 of the third, but the Senators successfully challenged that the Blackhawks were offside, and the goal was overturned. The announcement that the challenge was successful was not met with much joy from the packed United Center, but Bedard admitted after the game that he knew it probably wasn't going to stay on the board.

It was OK, though. Jason Dickinson scored what would hold up as the game-winning goal with less than two minutes remaining in regulation. The Blackhawks' eight-game losing skid was over and Bedard had jumped back into the highlight packages across North America with his performance.

Dickinson's goal was the kind that the Blackhawks were struggling to score. He got a couple whacks at a rebound and was in the process of getting tripped to the ground as he finally slid it into the net. It wasn't nearly as pretty as Bedard's goal, but it counted when the Blackhawks needed it most.

Bedard was named the First Star of the game and received a thunderous ovation from the sold-out building. It had been a long time since Blackhawks fans could cheer for a victory. This was their first win in almost a full calendar month. (Their previous win was on January 19; this one came on February 17).

"It's great," Bedard said after the win. "Especially getting back and being at home for a couple games and getting to kind of feel that energy and stuff. It's awesome. To get a win, it's been a long time for myself. I think we were on a five-game losing streak when I was playing and obviously it's hard watching, and it's hard watching when we're losing, so it feels good for all of us to get that."

After the game, Dickinson was asked about how veterans like him seemingly had more jump in their game because an 18-year-old had joined the lineup. He admitted that the excitement transcended the stands at the United Center and did indeed influence their play on the ice.

"Everybody knows he's a dynamic player, he's electric with the puck," Dickinson said. "You give him opportunities [and] he's gonna make something happen and it brings a lot more depth to the lineup, a lot more danger to that line. So teams have to think a little bit harder.

"Not too often does an 18-year-old come in and have this kind of an impact on a team. It's very few players that have the opportunity to do something like that, and it's even fewer that take that opportunity and run with it. He's a special player, demands a lot of himself and it shows in his play. He's going out there and making it happen."

Foligno echoed those comments.

"We go as he goes a lot of nights," Foligno said. "Off the rush, he's so dangerous. It's nice to have a guy like that, that's thinking that way. A lot of times, we're chipping it in with a lunch pail attitude, and he's a guy that can make those plays and catch teams off-guard…. Those are the plays that you miss and are excited to see start going in for him."

After the win, Richardson was also complimentary of his young superstar, who appeared to only need one period to kick off 41 days of rust.

"He's a special player," Richardson said. "Like, when Sidney Crosby was that age, I'm sure it had the same effect. [Connor]

McDavid. And you can go on and on with those special players. Connor's got that effect, not just with the fans but, obviously, in the game itself."

The buzz was once again following Bedard, and fans didn't
need to wait long for another chance to watch him play.
However, the Blackhawks' next game was their only road contest of the entire month of February. And the Hawks were
heading to North Carolina to play one of the stingiest defensive
teams in the league. Bedard said the Blackhawks' 20-game road
losing streak was "embarrassing" before the team boarded a
plane to Raleigh, and they hoped to change that with an upset.

Before the game at Carolina, Richardson spoke with his
young players about how the Hurricanes aggressively hound
the puck and put constant pressure on players. He warned his
team that this would be a much tougher test than the games
against Pittsburgh or Ottawa—and he was right.

Carolina dominated the Blackhawks for the first 35 minutes
of the game. Bedard's line didn't see a single shot on net in
the first period. He did set up Foligno for the Blackhawks'
first goal at 15:23 into the second period, but the Blackhawks
were down 4–1 after that goal counted. When the dust settled for the second intermission, the Blackhawks were getting
outshot 31–9.

Late in the second period, Bedard was checked into
Carolina goaltender Spencer Martin. Martin gave him a shove
as he got away from the net and the period came to a close.
As the skaters made their way to their respective benches
after the horn, Martin whacked Bedard with his stick and
chirped him. Bedard responded with a whack of his own and
a few words for the goaltender. Foligno and Jarred Tinordi
shared a few kind words with some of Carolina's skaters before

everyone eventually made their way to their respective dressing rooms.

Early in the third period, the Canes hit Bedard a couple times, and he was tripped up on a play. Instead of getting frustrated, it appeared Bedard flipped a switch. He started to dominate the game.

After Carolina extended its lead to 5–1, it appeared Bedard scored Chicago's second goal. He ripped the shot over Martin and stood tall, staring down the goaltender who had chirped him between periods.

Unfortunately for the Blackhawks, another would-be Bedard goal would come off the board because they were offside; rookie defenseman Louis Crevier failed to keep the puck in the zone seconds before Bedard rifled the shot home. For the third time in the season and second time in as many games, Bedard had a goal taken away because of a review.

Bedard didn't appear to mind. Kurashev set him up on the doorstep moments later on a power play, and that goal counted. The Blackhawks were within three goals and Bedard had another multi-point game.

Two minutes later, on another power play, Bedard set up Tyler Johnson for an easy tap-in goal, and the Blackhawks had quickly cut the lead to 5–3. Bedard had been dominant for about six minutes and now had a three-point game.

That would be the end of Chicago's scoring, though. Carolina added an empty-net goal to make the final score 6–3. The loss made it 21 straight road games without a win for the Blackhawks.

Bedard didn't make much of the skirmish with Martin after the game. "It's hockey," he said. "I don't think it was anything too meaningful or whatever. It was funny. I'm always excited to play and stuff, but I think noticing how the game was going, I was kind of trying to be more physical or whatever and I guess I got in his face a little bit, which is fair. I don't think either of us are waking up and caring too much about it, but yeah, it's not a big deal at all."

Richardson noted that Bedard's reaction to Martin got his teammates excited and also took note of Bedard's increased effort to impact the game on the defensive end of the ice after his return from injury. The head coach pointed out a few times he put his head down and forced the action in the defensive end, calling it an improved part of his game.

Two nights later the Blackhawks had another stiff test waiting for them at the United Center. John Tortorella's Philadelphia Flyers were in town for a nationally televised game on TNT on a Wednesday night. And once again, the star rookie was asked to take time away from his pregame warm-up routine to put on a headset and speak with the studio crew of Liam McHugh, Anson Carter, Henrik Lundqvist, and Paul Bissonnette. Even though the Blackhawks were at the bottom of the NHL standings, the national television networks in the United States couldn't get enough of Bedard.

This was the first time Bedard would play on national television in the U.S. since his jaw injury, so the questions focused on his rehab process and how he stayed game-ready during his 41 days out of game action. Bisonnette also asked about his relationship with Nick Foligno, which gave Bedard another opportunity to praise his veteran teammate and the de facto Blackhawks captain for how much he had meant to the young guys in the room during the season.

"He's been unreal. We're so lucky to have him and a lot of guys showing us the ropes," Bedard said. "For us young guys, we came in and we felt so comfortable and he's someone that I think every game has some tips or whatever and it's really helped me and a lot of us."

Bedard wasn't quite as kind to his elder teammate later in the night, however. Turner put its "Active Mic" on Bedard at one point on the bench and shared a brief video clip of him talking through a play with Foligno. Foligno asked if he thought he was getting the puck back, to which Bedard answered, "You were just slow." They talked about the play for another couple seconds in the clip before the network cut forward to Foligno asking Bedard, "Are you calling me slow?"

"No, I was saying you were going slow," Bedard replied.

"You're pissing me off," Foligno said as he turned his attention to the ice with a smile. Bedard laughed.

That kind of playful back-and-forth had been a hallmark of their camaraderie on the ice and in the room from the time Bedard arrived in Chicago. And the cameras catching it gave fans around the U.S. an inside look at their relationship for about 15 seconds.

Bedard came into the game with six points in three games since returning to the team; Foligno and Philipp Kurashev had points in all six Blackhawks games since the All-Star Game. That line was really the only one driving offense for the team, so they naturally got their share of attention from Tortorella's defense.

During the game, Bedard got a one-on-one rush against Flyers defenseman Nick Seeler. As he attacked, Bedard gave the defender's stick a whack out of the way before passing the puck back between his own legs to his backhand, from which he attempted a shot that just missed. The play got the

United Center on its feet on an otherwise modest offensive night from the Hawks.

When asked about the move later, Bedard said his good friend Andrew Cristall (who was drafted in the second round by the Washington Capitals in 2023) had pulled it off in junior while playing for Kelowna when they were both in the WHL, and he just saw an opportunity to try it.

"Just kind of in the moment, see what you've got. It's rare that you get a clean one-on-one like that so I just thought I would give it a try," Bedard said with a smile. "I watched it and he didn't really move or anything."

The Blackhawks' next game might have been the most overlooked on the entire season schedule for fans and media alike. The players needed to focus on a tough, strong Winnipeg Jets team coming into Chicago; everyone else was more concerned with the events ahead on that Sunday, when the Blackhawks would retire Chris Chelios' jersey and Patrick Kane would return to Chicago for the first time as a visitor.

Bedard started fielding questions about Kane's return days before that game. He respectfully answered, but tried to stay focused on the Jets. Chicago had played Winnipeg tough in their first three meetings, including Bedard scoring an overtime game-winner against the Jets just after Christmas. The hope in the Blackhawks' room was that they could finish for a second time against a playoff team to build some momentum.

For the third time in four meetings, this game was decided by one goal. The Blackhawks lost 3–2 in overtime—an overtime that lasted only 25 seconds and didn't see Bedard even get on the ice. Many questioned the decision to leave Bedard on the bench in a close game to start overtime, but Blackhawks coach Luke Richardson said they were focused on winning the opening faceoff and forcing the Jets' top forwards to play defense to start the extra session before sending Bedard out. Unfortunately, he never got that chance.

Bedard's personal point streak came to an end with the Jets' loss. For the first time since returning from injury, he failed to make a dent in the box score.

With the Winnipeg game in the books, the attention on the Blackhawks started to turn up around Chicago. Their next game would be one of the marquee events on the entire city's sports calendar for the year.

CHAPTER 9

1 ON 1

"I'M JUST PUMPED FOR THE VIDEO TRIBUTE. I think it's going to be pretty nasty. He had some sick highlights here. I've watched every one of his mix tapes probably 100 times, with his stuff. I'm pumped for that. For him, it's going to be a pretty special night with Cheli getting the jersey, too. It's going to be a cool night, for sure."

Sunday, February 25, was a date many Blackhawks fans had circled on their calendars all the way back on September 7. That night, at a Pearl Jam concert at the United Center, the Blackhawks surprised Hall of Fame defenseman Chris Chelios on stage as frontman Eddie Vedder told him his No. 7 was going to be retired by the franchise when the Blackhawks hosted the Detroit Red Wings.

Detroit games in Chicago have been special for almost 100 years. The rivalry runs deep, all the way back to Arthur Wirtz having a partial ownership stake in the Red Wings before buying the Blackhawks. Fans don't like each other, players have often hated each other, and things have been known to get as heated in the stands as they do on the ice.

But in 1999, the Blackhawks traded Chelios to Detroit in a deal that became instantly infamous. The Chicagoland native went on to win championships with the Wings, and the divorce between the Chicago team and fans and Chelios felt terribly final.

So announcing Chelios' name would be placed in the rafters with other icons of the franchise made this game a huge Chicago event.

Fast forward to November 29. The Red Wings were looking to add to their offense, and there was still a future Hall of Famer available. So Detroit signed Patrick Kane to a one-year contract.

Kane, the only player selected No. 1 overall by the Blackhawks before Bedard, would return to Chicago for the first time as a visitor on the same night the franchise honored another legend.

The hype around the game started weeks before the game itself with the Blackhawks finding unique ways to honor Chelios. The week of the game, the team announced Hall of Fame voice of the Blackhawks Pat Foley would return to host a panel discussion about Chelios' career with a few of his former teammates. Jeremy Roenick, Eddie Belfour, Denis Savard, Tony Amonte, and Gary Suter were all coming back to the United Center to take part in the night. Later in the week, Chelios told 670 The Score in Chicago that Michael Jordan planned to be at the game. (He was ultimately unable to attend.)

Bedard versus Kane in front of those dignitaries and Chicago legends made this an even bigger night on the season calendar for everyone.

It was special for Bedard, too. Kane had reached out via phone call after the draft to congratulate him for becoming the second No. 1 overall pick in franchise history. Bedard didn't necessarily want to start hearing more about the comparisons of the two and the idea of living up to Kane's presence in Chicago, but he praised one of the players who had brought the Blackhawks franchise back from the depths of the league to become a dynasty.

"I don't care too much what people say behind the scenes. If I can be anything like him, that's pretty great, with the career he had. I'm my own person and player and everything, so I'll do what I do, and he does what he does. He's had a special career, of course, but it's hard to compare two guys I think."

Bedard was asked a couple days before the game if the schedule of events—with a ceremony beginning almost two hours before puck drop—was going to mess with his routine at all. "Not at all, really. That's part of being professional and you have to prepare no matter the circumstances." A modest answer—one that might have come from Kane, not the 18-year-old seemingly following in his footsteps as the most exciting player at 1901 W. Madison Street in Chicago.

The hype around the event grew with the Red Wings—and Kane—coming in playing very well. There were a lot of emotions for Blackhawks fans of all ages with the confluence of celebrating Chris Chelios' career, celebrating the return of Kane, and the hope for the future with Bedard.

Kane spoke with Chicago media for the first time since he had been traded to the New York Rangers—almost exactly one full year prior—early the morning of the game at the Ritz-Carlton hotel, where the Red Wings were staying. Because of the events at the United Center and the Red Wings playing the day before, there was no time closer to the game for him to speak about his return.

It was clear that Kane was still trying to figure out what his emotions would be when he walked into the visitors' dressing room for the first time, and then when he took the ice in the wrong jersey for the first time. But he was clear in his praise of Bedard, whom he would face for the first time.

"He's been amazing. He's been great," Kane said. "We talk about the fans and the city and how it's such a great sports town—he's in a great spot for that. I think the fans deserve another long run of a great hockey player and hopefully great teams behind him. But I think it's a great way to kind of, I said this the other day, start the rebuild and to start with a player like that definitely accelerates it a little bit. But he's been special. I'm sure you guys see it covering him every night. He's worth the price of admission. He does special things. He's going to be a great player for a long time."

When asked what he appreciates about Bedard's game from watching him as a rookie, Kane was complimentary again.

"I think obviously he has so much skill and his shot, very creative out there, but when I think about him, I think about the work you have to put in to be at that level, right? Some people think it's God-given talent or things like that. You go through it yourself when you're younger…. That's what I think with Connor. It seems he loves the game, loves practicing, loves working at his game. So all that stuff pays off."

That afternoon when he arrived for the game, Bedard was wearing a black Blackhawks Chelios sweater with a "C" on the chest. All the Blackhawks' players arrived in Chelios apparel, either jerseys or T-shirts or sweatshirts. And they all kept the shirts on as they took the bench to watch his jersey retirement ceremony.

On the other bench, the entire Red Wings team and coaching staff also sat on their bench to show appreciation for one of the greatest American-born players in NHL history.

While speaking on the ice, Chelios mentioned Kane by name, saying he was taking the mantle as the greatest American-born player in the NHL. Chelios tried to not make too big of a deal out of Kane now being a Red Wing as he once was, but did ask that Kane not steal his thunder on the night his No. 7 was put in the rafters forever.

Chelios always knew how to throw a party, and his friendship circle has always cast a wide net. He had a lot of celebrities in attendance for the game, including tennis great John McEnroe, NBA Hall of Famer and former Chicago Bull Dennis Rodman, Pearl Jam frontman Eddie Vedder, supermodel Cindy Crawford, and former Cubs and Boston Red Sox executive Theo Epstein.

Also in the suite for Chelios' retirement ceremony were two of the NHL's all-time greats—Wayne Gretzky and Mark Messier. Before the game, Gretzky made a stop in the Blackhawks' dressing room to speak with Bedard for some time.

"I talked to him pretty briefly, but I'm fortunate to have talked to him a couple of times now and feel comfortable having a conversation with him, which is obviously cool," Bedard said about his conversation with the Great One. "He is the best player ever and the impact he has…. I think how much he cares about that and how much he accepts that role is pretty impressive."

There was a lot of "greatest" talk around the United Center that night, but Bedard thinking about how Gretzky carries the mantle of being the undisputed greatest to ever play the game at the NHL level was another reminder of how he paid attention to things that weren't necessarily focused wholly on a person's on-ice impact.

After the ceremony ended, the two teams had to get focused on actually playing a game. That task was undoubtedly easier for the Blackhawks and most of the Red Wings than it was for Kane, who knew there would be a tribute video for him during the first television timeout.

When the video played early in the game, the roar from the reported 21,141 fans in attendance was deafening. Kane took a lap out on the ice with his stick raised high to thank the Chicago faithful for the applause. He then took a second lap. And, finally, a third. Fittingly, one lap for each championship he won with the Chicago Blackhawks.

The Blackhawks tapped their sticks on their bench and on the ice just as Kane's Red Wings teammates did throughout the nearly three-minute ovation. The love that poured down for the hero was loud and well received.

But, again, after the three laps on the ice, the game needed to go on. And it did.

The Red Wings took a 1–0 lead late in the first period. Chicago played well in the opening 20 minutes but went to the room down one. The Blackhawks came out with more energy in the second period and scored twice, the second of which came on the power play. Bedard ripped a shot on net that was redirected by Nick Foligno past James Reimer for the go-ahead goal.

During the second period, Bedard and Kane were on the ice together briefly; Chicago tried to get its best defensive forward line on the ice against Kane's line as much as possible. That didn't stop Bedard from putting a big hit on Kane in the corner, appearing to stagger the elder superstar a bit. The highlight hit social media and started a blaze of comments about Bedard playing Kane physically.

As he had so many times with the Blackhawks throughout his career, Kane knew how to finish a game. Late in the
third period, he set up the other former Blackhawk scorer on
Detroit's roster, Alex DeBrincat, for a tying goal.

And the script was set—Blackhawks and Red Wings heading to overtime.

Bedard started overtime on the ice for the Blackhawks this
time, a change from the Hawks' approach two days earlier
against Winnipeg.

Detroit was able to get Kane on the ice as the puck moved
around the ice. Seth Jones had a chance to attack the net
and took it but wasn't able to finish. Waiting for a breakaway
behind the three Blackhawks on the ice: Kane. He had a one-
on-one with Petr Mrázek and, like so many shootout chances
he'd had over the years, buried it.

The United Center erupted in surreal excitement. The
Blackhawks lost the game, but the prodigal son had dramatically ended it. Kane raised both hands to the sky and shouted
at the stands as Blackhawks and Red Wings fans cheered. The
Detroit bench emptied and mobbed him on the opposite end
of the ice as the Blackhawks all left the ice and retreated to
their dressing room.

As the Red Wings left the ice, Kane slapped a high five or
hugged each teammate in front of the Detroit bench. As his
final teammate made it to the bench, Kane took one more
lap around the United Center ice. He tapped his heart and
pointed to the crowd again. The broadcast showed his parents
cheering, a familiar sight at the United Center.

After the game, more Chicago media poured into the
visitors' dressing room to speak with Kane than waited for
the Blackhawks' room to open. Kane spoke about the hype,

the nostalgia, and the emotions of the night. And skating against Bedard for the first time.

When asked about Bedard's big hit on him, Kane cracked his familiar smile and chuckled. "[He] got a little physical on me in the corner there, so I was lucky he had the bubble on, or I was going after him."

That chirp from Kane made its way around social media that night and in the days that followed. Bedard had a good laugh at it as well.

"I'm pretty sure he wasn't too serious," Bedard said. "I heard that, and I thought it was pretty funny.... Obviously he got the last laugh on us, but it was good to kind of hear that joking about it."

Everything about the night was historic for Chicago sports and the Blackhawks organization. Everything except getting a win. Bedard played well and picked up an assist. He stepped up and played physically against the only other player in Blackhawks history to be selected No. 1 overall. But, in the end, he was left with another (as Bedard would say) sick highlight of Kane's career being added to the books.

CHAPTER 10

LOSING SUCKS

A S THE CALENDAR NEARED MARCH, the Blackhawks were sitting in last place in the NHL. But Bedard business was still booming for the organization. Three months into the fiscal year for the 2023–24 season, the Blackhawks had nearly doubled their total merchandise sales compared with the same time frame for the previous year.

According to the team, the Blackhawks were consistently selling hundreds of Bedard jerseys per home game still through February. Of those sales, approximately 85 percent were authentic jerseys and 15 percent replica jerseys. And the team did not report any slowdown in sales while he was out of the lineup for six weeks.

The Bedard Boom was helping the overall bottom line well beyond jersey sales, too. The team reported a 52 percent increase in year-to-date retail sales at all team-managed locations, and their average game-day revenue was up 72 percent from the previous season.

While the business side of the house was benefiting, the on-ice product needed a boost. The Blackhawks had three days between games following the loss to the Red Wings to digest that day's events and collect themselves. That defeat put the Hawks' record at 4–16–3 since the calendar had turned to the new year, and it didn't go without notice that the struggle to win games was taking its toll on the room.

Luke Richardson gave the team Monday off before getting back on the ice for a couple days of practice. The Colorado Avalanche were coming into the United Center for a game on Thursday night—a rare leap-year night game on February 29— that would be nationally televised on ESPN. The headline matchup of Bedard against Nathan MacKinnon was the easy selling point for viewers, but the Blackhawks were still trying to find the right formula to win games.

"Losing sucks," Bedard said after that Wednesday practice. "No one enjoys losing. We have a lot of pride as professional athletes and it's, it's hard. Losing games is no fun. So I mean, yeah, it's been tough sometimes for sure. But I think we're just trying to stay as positive we can and grow and obviously take a step here in the last bit of the season."

The matchup with MacKinnon wasn't lost on Bedard, though. The two had spent some time together in Toronto at the All-Star Game, and the cameras caught MacKinnon grabbing one of Bedard's sticks and looking at it. There did seem to be a bit of a fascination with Bedard playing with a 70-flex stick. During the skills competition in which he was able to participate, Bedard was selected to be the passer for three skaters in the one-timer contest, including MacKinnon—who won the event.

After the event, MacKinnon spoke highly of Bedard's skill. The Blackhawks had beaten the Avalanche 3–2 the last time the two teams played in Chicago, all the way back on December 19. Bedard had two assists in that game. After

Chicago's morning skate, Bedard didn't mince words when asked what he liked about MacKinnon's game. When asked what about MacKinnon's game stood out, Bedard ran his fingers through his hair and said, "Everything."

"He's so fast and so powerful and thinks the game so well. There are only so many guys who can move that fast but also think at that pace and at that speed and his hands move along with him. He's one of my favorite players to watch. Just every shift I feel like there's something going and it's exciting hockey. Obviously, he's probably one of the top candidates for MVP so far this year."

MacKinnon came into the game in Chicago with 98 points on the season. The Blackhawks came out of the gates with a much better start than some other recent games and actually carried the play for the opening 18 minutes. But, as had been the issue for the Blackhawks all season, the first little mistake ended up in the back of the net and the floodgates opened.

A turnover inside the final two minutes of the first period resulted in a Zach Parise goal that gave the Avalanche a 1–0 lead. The game was close through the opening period; it was not in the second. Colorado scored twice in 42 seconds early in the middle period and then got a third goal inside the final two seconds of the frame to take a 4–0 lead to the room. MacKinnon had one assist heading to the third period. His 36th goal of the season at 17:32 into the third period gave him an even 100 points for the season.

To those outside Chicago, a dominant 5–0 final score from a Colorado team that had come into the game struggling was likely an expected result. And the headlines at a league level were focused on MacKinnon reaching the century mark for the second consecutive year.

But those who watched the game in Chicago were concerned with the amount of harassment Bedard was taking without much recourse from other Blackhawks. Josh Manson, whose father, Dave, played for the Blackhawks, slashed Bedard across the hands at one point, causing the rookie to drop his stick and shake his hands in pain. Later in the third period, Manson and Bedard exchanged slashes in the corner and Manson held Bedard from skating away. No penalties were called at any point during the action.

After the game, Blackhawks players and coaches were asked about the amount of hits Bedard was taking for the second straight game. Jarred Tinordi, one of the team's "enforcers," said he didn't see the slash. Neither did Reese Johnson, who did drop the gloves with Chris Wagner during the game for a rousing fight.

Luke Richardson said he also didn't see the slash. But he did sense his team was showing more internal frustration as the losses continued to pile up. Goaltender Petr Mrázek appeared to stare at defenseman Jaycob Megna after Colorado's second goal in the game. There were also a few incidents where it appeared Blackhawks were barking at each other on the bench as the goals were added to the wrong side of the scoreboard. Richardson acknowledged it was tough on the players to not come up short this time, but get their doors blown off by a much better team.

"I think this team has been really good about talking about things and coming to the rink the next day with a good atti-tude to work," the Blackhawks head coach said after the game. "And that's what we'll have to do. It's a scheduled day off for the players tomorrow in the month. Maybe it's good to get away and just think about something else and come back

Saturday morning ready to have a quick morning skate and get ready for a team that we want to come in and end our homestand on a real good note. Because now we're going to start traveling a little bit and we want to make sure that we create and maintain that good atmosphere here."

For Bedard, more physical play wasn't necessarily a surprise, even though he was coming back from a fairly significant injury. "I don't think it's really been that crazy, to be honest with you," he said. "It's hockey. It's physical. If it does happen, just keep playing my game and I think sometimes that's nice, gets you in the game a bit."

The Blackhawks did take the day off after the Colorado loss to regroup and then returned to the ice at the United Center for a morning skate on a beautiful Saturday in early March. The sun was shining in Chicago, the temperature was going to be in the low 60s Fahrenheit, and the Blackhawks were hosting their final home game in a span that saw them host 10 of 11 games at the United Center after the All-Star break.

Visiting the Windy City on that Saturday were the Columbus Blue Jackets, who were chasing the Blackhawks to the bottom of the standings. Unfortunately for those who bought tickets hoping to see a matchup of two of the top three overall picks in the 2023 NHL Draft, Adam Fantilli was not in the lineup for Columbus.

Fantilli had suffered a laceration to his lower left leg in a game in Seattle near the end of January. The Blue Jackets were also without young forwards Kent Johnson and Patrik Laine, who was in the NHL/NHLPA Player Assistance Program.

If not being able to see the potential matchup of Fantilli and Bedard took some of the luster off the game before it started, the Blackhawks' performance on the ice left plenty to be desired. It was the worst game the Blackhawks played during a stretch in which they played 10 of 11 games on their home ice; they came out flat and never matched the intensity of a struggling Blue Jackets team.

The Blackhawks were getting outworked and outhustled for most of the first period. But Bedard's line, which saw Ryan Donato added late in the Colorado loss and to start this game, was able to generate some offense late in the first period. Bedard and Donato got physical behind the net, with Bedard hitting Alex Nylander to knock a puck loose. Donato got the puck back to Bedard, who found Philipp Kurashev alone in front of the net for an easy goal.

Unfortunately for the Hawks, Columbus took a 4–1 lead to the third period. Donato scored early in the third, but that was the end of the offense for Chicago. The Blue Jackets got physical with Bedard just as the Avalanche had, but he played through the whacks and trips. He finished the game leading Blackhawks forwards in ice time at 21:19 with an assist on Kurashev's goal and a forward-leading two blocked shots. But he failed to win any of his seven faceoffs in the game.

It was another disheartening loss for a Blackhawks team that was starting to show its frustration more frequently. After the game, Kurashev and Donato repeated the phrase that Bedard had used too often since returning from his jaw injury: "Losing sucks."

The Blackhawks played 10 games—nine at home—in 22 days in February following the All-Star break. They won only once. And they started March with a dull thud against a team they, at least on paper, had much better odds of competing with in the Blue Jackets.

Their stretch of home games was done now, and the Hawks hit the road for back-to-back nights against the Avalanche and Coyotes to start a new week. After not facing Colorado for more than two months, the Blackhawks would play them twice in five days; the Hawks would play in Arizona on Tuesday and then host the Coyotes five days later.

Maybe getting on the road would help the Blackhawks mentally reset after playing so many games at home, but Chicago hadn't won a road game since November 9 in Tampa. "I mean, we don't think about it much but obviously it's pretty embarrassing," Bedard said before the team left Chicago. "It's a long time and obviously we want to end that for sure."

The season was now three-quarters of the way done for the team, a time when some rookies—especially teenage rookies—start to feel the weight of the long NHL season. But Bedard gave credit to the team's training staff and Paul Goodman for a good regimen to keep him feeling strong into March.

Bedard was feeling good and playing well, and the first full week of March brought another first for his NHL career. The NHL's trade deadline was 3:00 PM ET on Friday, March 8, and Bedard was being asked questions about the possibility that veteran leaders like Tyler Johnson or Colin Blackwell might be leaving.

Meanwhile, Upper Deck was set to start shipping its Series II hockey cards for the 2023–24 season. Included in that portion of their set was Bedard's "Young Guns" rookie card—his first premium card in a Blackhawks jersey. On March 4, one collectibles shop, Dave & Adam's Card World in New York, tweeted a $1 million bounty for Bedard's "Outburst Gold 1/1 Young Guns" card. A one-of-one print of a generational rookie's card had a $1 million offer before the packs were even starting to get ripped. Even the NHL's website had a story about the hype around Bedard's rookie cards finally hitting the market.

Bedard admitted he collected hockey cards when he was younger, and thought it was cool that he would now be on an NHL card.

"I have a big binder at home, so I guess it's cool to kind of be on one now," Bedard said.

With increasing talk on social media about the release of Bedard's rookie cards, the Blackhawks hit the road for their back-to-back games against the Avalanche and Coyotes. After getting shut out 5–0 at home by the Avs, the Hawks got another look at them four days later in Denver. The hope was that the Blackhawks would bring better energy to the ice and end their 21-game road losing streak.

After closing their long homestand with two ugly losses in which they were outscored 10–2, the Blackhawks talked about wanting to get off to a better start. And being on the road would give them a fresh approach. In theory.

The Colorado team that had played the Blackhawks on the previous Thursday was without Josh Manson, who was a scratch. Manson had hit Bedard a few times and there was a lot of talk about his slash across Bedard's hands in the game in Chicago. Bedard downplayed the incidents, saying it was all part of the game. His teammates and coaches did, too. But that didn't stop the fans and media from talking about how much harassment the phenom was taking on the ice after returning from six weeks on the shelf.

Unfortunately for the Blackhawks, this game against the Avalanche was far too similar to the one in Chicago—except the Hawks did not come out strong and outplay Colorado for the first portion of the game.

The Blackhawks were totally flat in this game from start to finish. Colorado took a two-goal lead in the first period and extended that to four in the second. The game ended with the same 5–0 score as the disappointing loss four days earlier.

Five minutes into the second period, Bedard got a breakaway chance with the Blackhawks down two goals. He attacked but wasn't quite able to finish. As the Colorado goaltender froze the puck, Bedard hunched over in frustration and looked to the sky for an answer—and to watch the replay on the scoreboard.

It was that kind of night for all the Blackhawks. After the game, Seth Jones was more visibly agitated by the lack of coordinated effort from the team. There was growing, open frustration from the Blackhawks as losses continued to pile up.

Chicago had dropped seven straight games heading to the desert to face an Arizona team that had gone winless in February. Even the Blackhawks had won one game in the calendar month. But the Coyotes started March with two wins, and they put eight goals on the Blackhawks the last time the two teams played.

Bedard was struggling to produce as much as any of his teammates. He had some great opportunities, including the breakaway in Denver, but hadn't been able to convert. In the Blackhawks' six games before playing in Arizona, Bedard had only two assists to show for 14 shots on goal. He was still playing heavy minutes, but the Blackhawks hadn't scored more than two goals in a game since Bedard's three-point effort in a 6–3 loss to Carolina on February 19.

After the Blackhawks players had some tough internal conversations following the blowout loss in Denver, the start in Arizona was better. Chicago was moving the puck better, playing better team defense, and getting opportunities. When the Blackhawks got a 5-on-3 power play in the middle of the first period, they were able to finally score the first goal in a game; they hadn't done that since their last win 17 days prior against the Ottawa Senators.

What's more, Bedard set up Jones for the power play goal—the first power-play marker from a Blackhawks defenseman in the entire season. There was instant energy from the Blackhawks' bench, and the team dominated the rest of the first period to take a one-goal lead to the first intermission.

Arizona tied the game early in the second period, but the Blackhawks quickly got a second power play. Bedard set up Nick Foligno for a goal this time, and Chicago took the lead back. Two power play goals in a game for the Blackhawks felt like a weight had been lifted.

Seven minutes after the Blackhawks' second goal, the Coyotes tied the game again. But the Blackhawks did not show the same frustration or defeated body language they had in so many recent games. Chicago got another power play and converted again. When the Blackhawks scored a fourth power play goal in the closing minutes of the second period, it felt like the stars were aligned.

The Blackhawks scored the only goal of the third period, an empty-net goal from Jones, to close out a 5–2 win. Chicago dominated the game from start to finish, and a lot of guys on the roster put negative streaks to bed.

The Blackhawks organization hadn't scored four power play goals in a single game in more than six years. Bedard's two assists gave him 10 points in 10 games since returning from injury. The team vibe in the room was one of both happiness and relief that the longest road losing streak in franchise history was finally over, and the offense had clicked for the first time in weeks.

"Oh my God, that was a long time," a smiling Bedard said after the game. "It's good. Obviously, you try not to think about it much, but that was a pretty crazy stretch there. It's nice that that's over. The first happy plane ride we've had in a little bit."

The Blackhawks were on a three-game trip that saw them travel from Denver to the desert of Arizona and then across the country to the capital of the United States, where they would face the Washington Capitals four days later. After a brief day of practice at home, the Blackhawks headed to DC for an early start against Alexander Ovechkin and the Caps.

After ending their road losing skid, the Hawks hoped they could continue their solid play. That, unfortunately, was not the case. Washington took a three-goal lead in the opening 14 minutes of the game and put the game in cruise control. Chicago was able to score once in the third period—at which point it was trailing by four—but the game was another lackluster performance after such a strong effort against the Coyotes earlier in the week.

However, in the midst of a mediocre performance by the team as a whole, Bedard showed something that hadn't been as outwardly visible previously in his NHL career. He was clearly frustrated by the lack of scoring; the Blackhawks couldn't solve Charlie Lindgren, the Capitals' netminder, despite plenty of chances.

During the second and third periods, but especially the third, Bedard appeared to make it his mission to get the Blackhawks back in the game. He was trying to will goals into being. At one point he stopped on a dime and maneuvered the puck around a defender, and then pulled off the same move on another before looking for a trailing teammate to get a shot on net. The move received an audible "wow" from the crowd in Washington.

When the dust settled from an underwhelming 4–1 loss, Bedard was credited with 16 shot attempts in the game. It was as intentionally forceful as he had been since returning from his injury—perhaps in the entire season.

Richardson said he liked the confidence with which Bedard was playing and wanted to see more of it.

His wish was granted the following day when, less than 22 hours after their game ended in Washington, the puck dropped at the United Center for an early-evening game against the same Coyotes team the Blackhawks had beaten soundly earlier in the week.

After being thoroughly demolished in their own barn, the Coyotes did not get the memo that they were supposed to lose with relative ease again. The Coyotes took a one-goal lead to the room for the first intermission and scored a second goal, both from Clayton Keller, just 11 seconds into the second period. Not exactly an ideal script for the Blackhawks.

Bedard was on the ice for both of Arizona's goals, and it was apparent he wasn't happy to be chasing a couple early in the second period. As he had in Washington, the teenager took it upon himself to change his team's fortunes. And this time, the shots went in.

He scored the Blackhawks' first goal of the second period awkwardly, appearing to bank a pass attempt from behind the net off a defender's shins or skate and into the net. The goal ended an eight-game goalless streak for Bedard. He wasn't done, though.

After Colin Blackwell tied the game at two less than two minutes after Bedard's first goal, the phenom scored a power play goal to give the Blackhawks a 3–2 lead. Arizona tied the game, but Bedard then set up Tyler Johnson for another power play goal inside the final three minutes of the second period to put Chicago back on top. The assist gave Bedard three points in the second period.

Chicago would outscore Arizona 3–1 in the third period to skate away with a stunning 7–4 victory. Blackwell recorded his first career hat trick, and Bedard nearly had his. The two, who each had two goals at the time, had a two-on-one break-away in the third period. Blackwell sauced the pass across the offensive zone to Bedard for a great scoring chance, but the shot went just wide.

After the game, Bedard could joke about missing out on his first career hat trick. "If I was any good, I'd put it in," Bedard said with a smirk. "But unfortunately it slid off."

Following his career-high 16 shot attempts in Washington, Bedard came back with 13 more the following afternoon, seven of which were on net (tying his career high).

"It's frustrating," Bedard said about his recent struggles to score after the game. "As an offensive guy I want to produce, and I think I probably had better games than this one where it wasn't going in, but it's nice to get a couple tonight for sure."

The seven goals scored by the Blackhawks were the most in a game to date in the season. In 12 games since returning from his jaw injury, Bedard was up to four goals and nine assists—better than a full point-per-game pace. And he had been credited with 37 shots on goal, more than three per game.

Two nights later, the Anaheim Ducks visited the United Center. Leo Carlsson, the No. 2 overall pick in the 2023 draft, was still out of the Ducks' lineup because of injury. Anaheim came into the game with the third-worst record in the league, better than only Chicago and San Jose.

Following their seven-goal outburst against the Coyotes, the Blackhawks came out firing against the Ducks. Chicago got the first power play of the game and scored while it had the advantage. Unfortunately, the Ducks scored a short-handed goal on the same power play, so the Hawks' goal tied the game at one. After 20 minutes, the Blackhawks had outshot the Ducks 18–9, but the score was tied at one.

As was the case against Arizona, Anaheim scored quickly in the second period to take a 2–1 lead. And then the Blackhawks—especially Bedard—took off. Bedard set up Philipp Kurashev for a game-tying goal less than two minutes after the Ducks took the lead. He was credited with the second assist on a Seth Jones power play goal later in the period. And he made a strong play on the puck to create a scoring chance for himself that he converted with 29 seconds remaining in the period.

The Blackhawks took a 4–2 lead to the dressing room, and Bedard had another three-point period on his young résumé.

In this game, the Blackhawks would outscore their opponent 3–0 in the third period to skate away with a dominant 7–2 win. Bedard picked up a third assist on a Kurashev power play goal and a fourth on a Tyler Johnson power play goal later in the third period, giving him his first career five-point game.

During the game and after, the NHL's social media channels were flooded once again with Bedard highlights and historic benchmarks. He was once again doing things hockey fans hadn't seen in generations—if ever.

The goal was Bedard's 20th of his rookie season. The only other 18-year-old in Blackhawks history to reach 20 goals at that age was Eddie Olczyk, who scored 20 in 1984–85.

Bedard and Nick Foligno were both credited with four assists in the game, making them the first Blackhawks teammates with four assists each in a game since Steve Larmer and Jeremy Roenick on November 27, 1992.

The game was Bedard's fourth in which he recorded three points. The only other active players to record as many in a season as an 18-year-old were Sidney Crosby (11), Patrik Laine (5), and Jeff Skinner (5).

Bedard also became just the fifth 18-year-old in NHL history to record consecutive three-point games. The other four: Dale Hawerchuk, who did it three times during the 1981–82 season; Ron Francis during the 1981–82 season; Steve Yzerman in 1983–84; and Wayne Gretzky in 1979–80.

This was the second time during the season that Bedard had recorded four points in a game, making him only the sixth 18-year-old to have multiple four-point games at such a young age. The others: Hawerchuk (who did it four times), Crosby (three times), Bobby Carpenter (twice), Jack Hamilton (twice), and Gretzky (twice).

Bedard's three-point second period was the third instance of him putting three points on the board in a single period that season. Only one other 18-year-old in NHL history had three separate three-point periods (Ted Kennedy, who did it three times). Only two other 18-year-olds, Ilya Kovalchuk and Bobby Carpenter, had multiple three-point periods before their 19th birthdays, and they did it only twice each.

Bedard became only the fifth 18-year-old in league history to have a five-point game, joining Ryan Nugent-Hopkins, Kovalchuk, Hawerchuk, and Hamilton. Previously, Nugent-Hopkins and Kovalchuk were the only other 18-year-olds with a four-assist game.

And Bedard joined Hawerchuk as the only teenager in NHL history to have eight points over a two-game span.

His personal heater had helped the Blackhawks win three out of four, a span during which they had outscored their opponents 20–12. However, the team that waited next on the schedule wasn't Arizona or Anaheim. The Los Angeles Kings were coming to Chicago with a collection of big centers and physical players all over their lineup.

This would be the first time Bedard would get a chance to skate against one of the big centers who had dominated the 2010s: Anže Kopitar. While Bedard wouldn't openly admit he got up for facing future Hall of Famers like Kopitar, he did note that it presented a challenge he welcomed.

Before the game against the Kings began, Bedard got to watch another Blackhawks skater take his celebratory rookie lap for the first time. Landon Slaggert, who had been the captain at Notre Dame during a strong senior season, had signed with the team earlier in the week and was set to make his NHL debut. Appropriately, the former Fighting Irish leader would join the team on the ice for an NHL game for the first time as the Blackhawks celebrated St. Patrick's Day in Chicago. His friends, former teammates, and family could wear their Notre Dame green and not stand out much in a crowd wearing green giveaway hats.

The challenge that night was staying hot against a Kings team that was fighting for playoff position in the Pacific Division. Unfortunately for Bedard and the Blackhawks, that order proved to be too tall.

LA scored four unanswered goals in the first period and showed its dominance for the full 60 minutes. When the dust settled, Bedard had skated 22:47—second on the team and the top ice time for a Chicago forward by more than four full minutes. But the Kings skated away with a 5–0 shutout victory.

Two nights later, the Blackhawks finished their three home games against the teams from California before heading west to face the same three teams in their home barns. The San Jose Sharks, the only team below the Blackhawks in the standings, came to Chicago for a battle against Bedard's Blackhawks.

After dominant wins against two other teams near the bottom of the standings during the week, the hope was that the Blackhawks could take advantage of a struggling Sharks team and get back in the win column. And many fans came to the United Center for an early Sunday-evening start with hopes that Bedard would put on another highlight-filled show.

The start of the game was far from what the Blackhawks wanted. San Jose took a 2–0 lead to the room for the first intermission; the Hawks did not come out firing as they had earlier in the week. And, after struggling against the Kings, it felt like there was some residual hangover from that beating.

In the second period, Bedard started a scoring play for Kurashev that got Chicago on the board. But the Blackhawks still trailed by one after 40 minutes of hockey.

It took 10 minutes in the third period for the dam to break against Sharks netminder Devin Cooley, who was making his

NHL debut, but when it did, the goals poured in. Ryan Donato scored at 10:39, Kevin Korchinski at 11:51, and Joey Anderson at 12:02 as the Blackhawks blitzed the rookie goalie to take a commanding 4–2 lead. Bedard scored into an empty net with less than one second showing on the clock to put a cap on a 5–2 comeback win. The goal gave Bedard 21 on the season and two points in the game.

Even with the shutout loss to the Kings in the middle of the week, Bedard had produced seven points in three games and was named the NHL's Second Star of the Week. In the NHL's press release, the league noted that Bedard's points-per-game rate of .98 ranked sixth among all rookies in the past 20 seasons (with a minimum of 40 games played).

Chicago was feeling pretty good for the first time during a long, injury-plagued season. Winners of four of their last six games, the Blackhawks now hopped on the team's charter and flew to California to face the Kings, Ducks, and Sharks again. Head coach Luke Richardson said he liked the quick turnaround against the three opponents because there were things the coaches were still trying to reinforce as they continued to emphasize development for their young players. And the familiarity with the three teams on the trip would give them an opportunity to change some things—or continue what had worked well.

The first game on the trip was in Los Angeles against the Kings team that had stymied Bedard and the rest of the Blackhawks offense just four days prior.

The first period in Los Angeles was a good one for the Blackhawks. The Kings took a 1–0 lead at 12:03 into the game, but the Blackhawks got a power play soon after and were able to convert a 5-on-3, with Nick Foligno handling the scoring.

After 20 minutes, the Blackhawks were tied with the Kings and looked like those changes the coaches had been preaching were taking effect. The second period showed the Hawks that the Kings still had the far superior roster.

LA scored three unanswered goals in the second period and dominated the Blackhawks. When Phillip Danault scored less than six minutes into the third period, the Blackhawks appeared to be done. But, to its credit, Chicago didn't quit. Bedard started a play that ended with Korchinski scoring his fifth goal of the season, a highlight he desperately needed. Korchinski and Jaycob Megna were on the wrong end of five of the Kings' six goals that night, and the youngest defenseman in the NHL looked the part.

Bedard led the team with six shot attempts again and picked up an assist on Korchinski's goal, but the loss was deflating after such a strong homestand. The Blackhawks had struggled on the road all year, and the first period was a glimpse of what they could do when committed. But the final 40 minutes were a painful reminder of how far they were from a playoff-caliber roster.

Two nights later the Blackhawks were in Anaheim to face the Ducks team they had beaten soundly at the United Center the previous week. This night would be just the second time Bedard would skate against Leo Carlsson, the second overall pick in the 2023 NHL Draft.

Unfortunately for the Ducks, Carlsson was involved in a collision with Alex Vlasic and left the game favoring his right leg.

Unfortunately for the Blackhawks, the effort that had previously earned them seven goals against the Ducks never got off the bus. The Ducks skated to a relatively easy 4–0 win,

Anaheim's first shutout victory of the season. Bedard put four shots on net in more than 20 more minutes of ice time, but the Blackhawks' road frustrations were showing again.

That loss led to a road trip conclusion in San Jose against a Sharks team the Blackhawks had blown out the previous weekend, although they needed to come back from a two-goal deficit to earn that lopsided win.

The Sharks called on Cooley again, his second start in the NHL. He allowed five unanswered goals in Chicago in his NHL debut. Six days later, he got a shot at redemption.

San Jose took the ice and the Blackhawks…waited to show up. Just as they had been in Anaheim, the Blackhawks were unorganized and flat for the first period. Thomas Bordeleau scored twice in the first 10:17 of the game and the Sharks took a two-goal lead to the room.

During the first period, the Blackhawks were bad enough that head coach Luke Richardson broke with his usually calm demeanor. During a television timeout early in the game, Richardson called his team together and lit them up.

"I didn't want to waste a timeout that early in the game," Richardson said. "I don't like doing that. But it just got to the point—and it didn't get much better right away, but I think it might take time to settle. I didn't really want to wait until the end of the first because it could trickle and get worse."

"When we feel like we've done our job and prepared them and we're doing the exact opposite of what our pregame message was and our video of the other team was, and they're doing the exact same thing they're doing, that's unprofessional and it's unacceptable," the head coach said. "I let them know that in the best way or fashion of urgency that I thought was needed at the time."

"It was a little scary," Ryan Donato said after the game. "Luke is a very kind guy, and when he needs to be, he can definitely get us going in the right direction if he needs to. He definitely did for us this game."

Richardson was right when he said it didn't get much better immediately after his "talk" to the team. As the broadcasters were beginning the period saying the Blackhawks had to be better, Fabian Zetterlund scored 16 seconds into the second. He scored again on a power play 84 seconds into the second to give the Sharks—the team with the worst record in the league—a four-goal lead after less than 22 minutes of hockey.

Richardson threw his lines in a blender to start the second period and one of those new lines started to click. Donato got the Blackhawks on the board at 6:45 into the second and then assisted on a Tyler Johnson goal seven minutes later. The Blackhawks were down 4–2 heading to the third period.

Bedard started a scoring play six minutes into the third period that cut the lead to one. With their own net empty, the Blackhawks were able to tie the game with 47 seconds left in regulation.

Chicago sent Bedard out with Philipp Kurashev and Seth Jones to start overtime, but it was Kurashev taking the faceoff. Bedard helped Kurashev win the faceoff, and Jones took his time attacking the offensive zone. Bedard crossed the ice and, understandably, got the attention of two of the three Sharks on the ice, opening a lane for Jones to get a good look. The shot was true, and the Blackhawks escaped San Jose with a 5–4 win after only 18 seconds of OT.

Bedard skated 22:47 in the game, once again more than four minutes more than any other Chicago forward. He put a team-leading six shots on net and picked up one assist in the game. It was the first time the Blackhawks had come back from a four-goal deficit in a game since a legendary game in October of 2009 against the Calgary Flames in which they trailed by five early in the game.

The historic comeback win wasn't all roses and champagne after the game, however. The Blackhawks traveled back to Chicago and had an off day on Sunday before jumping back on the ice at their practice rink on that Monday. It was a tough practice with physical drills that concluded with a bag skate; Richardson put his team through its paces at the end of the practice because even a four-goal comeback didn't erase the reality that they had played seven mediocre periods of hockey on the road trip after a strong homestand.

"I thought it was a full-team effort," Richardson said after that Monday practice, before cracking a bit of a smile. "A full-team effort the first half of the game to get into that trouble, then a full-team effort to get out of it. So, at least they all did it together."

With the Blackhawks coming home for a single game against the Calgary Flames before closing their March schedule on the road, Bedard's 21 goals were as many as Patrick Kane had scored in his rookie of the year effort during the 2007–08 season. His 55 points were one more than Jonathan Toews had produced that same season, when he finished third behind Kane and Washington's Nicklas Bäckström for the Calder Memorial Trophy.

Bedard was still learning and adjusting to the NHL life as an 18-year-old off the ice. He told Ben Pope of the *Chicago Sun-Times* that he still enjoyed going for walks and appreciated that Chicago people were respectful and nice and would occasionally say hi. And he said later that his comfort level both on and off the ice continued to grow as the season inched closer to its conclusion.

Teams were adjusting to Bedard's skill, and he was making adjustments to how teams approached him on the ice. His perspective remained focused on development in the midst of a lot of tough losses, but he was still working on changing results into wins for the Chicago Blackhawks.

CHAPTER 11

FINISHING A HISTORIC CAMPAIGN

"HE KNOWS WHAT TO DO with the puck and sometimes maybe he does a little too much with it.... With some of the wins lately, you've seen him at the end of games dumping pucks in and forechecking and being above the other team. That's huge growth."

The growth that Blackhawks head coach Luke Richardson spoke about before his team hosted the Calgary Flames on March 26—his 55th birthday—was continually evolving for Connor Bedard throughout his rookie season. As his linemates changed because of injuries, hot streaks, and other circumstances, Bedard was learning how to consistently take physical abuse, become more defensively responsible, and drive offense.

The one constant for Bedard over the second half of the regular season was linemate Philipp Kurashev. Entering the final week of March, Bedard had been on the ice with Kurashev for 803 minutes, 330-plus more minutes than any other forward on the Blackhawks roster. Kurashev, 24, was coming off two underwhelming seasons in which he had produced 46 points in 137 games. He had scored 15 goals and been credited with 31 assists over that span.

Moving onto a line with Bedard unlocked Kurashev's offense. He had started the season a little late because of an injury but had quickly developed chemistry on the ice and rapport off the ice with Bedard. The result: in 64 games, Kurashev had matched his 15 goals and 31 assists from the previous two seasons. And he was averaging a career-high 19 minutes per game.

The two had become a dynamic duo in the midst of a Blackhawks offense that struggled to score goals; they were responsible for 36 of the Blackhawks' 156 total goals as the Flames entered the United Center. And that number was with Bedard missing six weeks because of his broken jaw.

Bedard frequently complimented Kurashev's playmaking ability, something that had seemingly been an afterthought while he was spending most of the previous two years in more of a checking-line role. And Richardson spoke about Bedard unlocking Kurashev's hockey IQ; he finally had a linemate who elevated his game. Kurashev regularly spoke about how well the two complemented each other, and their production proved that to be evident many nights.

Their connection was on display early in the Blackhawks' game against the Flames coming off a bag skate by Richardson. The message was to compete, and the Hawks came out flying against Calgary. Chicago got a power play 47 seconds into the game and another to give them a two-man advantage 57 seconds later. Bedard was on the ice for 2:48 on the power play(s) that ended with him snapping a pass to Kurashev, who fed Seth Jones for the game's first goal.

Bedard came out firing, attempting six shots on the initial power play(s). He was credited with four of Chicago's 15 shots on net in the opening 20 minutes and skated almost nine minutes in the first period. The Blackhawks won the game 3–1, with two goals from Jason Dickinson. Bedard finished the night, once again, as the only Chicago forward to skate more than 20 minutes in the game (21:19) and was credited with five shots on net.

After finishing a home stretch in which the Blackhawks had played fairly well—four wins in five home games surrounding the three-game California trip—they hit the road for two games to close out the month of March. The first game would be Bedard's first in the capital city of Canada—Ottawa.

The Senators came into the 2023–24 season with high hopes, but their season had unraveled into another summer of early tee times and draft lottery watching. They had some veterans on their roster who played a heavy game, but the Blackhawks were winning games and felt good about their effort against the Flames.

That effort did not get off the bus in Ottawa. Chicago got a power play nine seconds into the game and allowed a short-handed goal 27 seconds later. The Senators scored a second goal six minutes into the game and that was it; the final score was 2–0.

Bedard was on the ice for both goals against and was frustrated by a mediocre first period. He struggled to get pucks on the net; he was credited with only two in the game. The Senators defense frustrated him as well; he had a team-worst three giveaways in the game.

The Blackhawks had played well at home and then their trip to California was bad. Richardson then put his team through a late-season bag skate to reset their thinking about the effort expected in the NHL and they responded with a strong game against the Flames. But this was a step in the wrong direction once again from a young team.

Chicago had one day off before its next game to consider the loss. The good news about the NHL schedule is, for better or worse, the next opportunity is always waiting.

The Blackhawks then traveled to Philadelphia for a Saturday-evening tilt against the Flyers. The Blackhawks coaches experimented a little with some different lines as the team played a totally flat game in Ottawa and opted to stay with those to start the game in Philly. The most significant change: Bedard on the wing.

Chicago's coaches moved Jason Dickinson, who was having a Selke Trophy–caliber season as one of the better defensive centers in the entire NHL, up to the top line with Bedard and Kurashev. The move was partially because Richardson wanted to see how his three best goal scorers performed together. It was also because he wanted to take some pressure off Bedard at the dot, with Dickinson being an excellent faceoff guy.

The move appeared to work. Dickinson won eight of 14 faceoffs in the game and led the Blackhawks with five hits. Bedard led the Blackhawks with six shots on net. He also picked up an assist. And the Blackhawks' other lines contributed to a strong offensive performance that ended with a 5–1 Blackhawks win.

Bedard's assist came on a Kurashev goal in the first period that gave Chicago a two-goal lead. The Blackhawks also got goals from Lukas Reichel, Nick Foligno—on the power play—Joey Anderson, and MacKenzie Entwistle. The goals were the fourth of the season for Reichel and Anderson and Entwistle's fifth of the campaign.

Chicago had now won six of its last 10 games and was starting to show a level of offensive chemistry it had lacked while dealing with so many injuries during the middle of the season. Bedard was still skating 20 minutes every night and was putting points on the board more nights than not, but scoring coming from the rest of the lineup was taking pressure off the 18-year-old to do it by himself.

When the Blackhawks practiced on Long Island on Monday after taking Easter Sunday off, Richardson noted that Bedard's move to the wing was not going to be a permanent thing, but an experiment he was hoping would help the rookie.

"We just felt like [it was] three smart hockey players," Richardson said. "It's just to get a good look at it. I liked the result last game. Not only did they score a nice rush goal, they created a few other [rushes] that we showed this morning on video and were good in the [defensive] zone.

"It's not necessarily [a] long-term [thing] for Connor, being on the wing. It's just sometimes where he starts out."

Bedard and Dickinson spent 11 minutes on the ice together in Philadelphia after spending only 26 minutes together the entire season before that game. Dickinson's defensive acumen complemented Bedard's playmaking ability; Bedard acknowledged he has a lot of work to do in the faceoff circle (he was winning 39 percent of his draws at the time) and appreciated that Dickinson was one of the better defensive centers in the entire NHL.

Before the Blackhawks started their April schedule against the New York Islanders, the NHL announced Bedard had been named the league's Rookie of the Month for his stellar performance in March. Bedard piled up 17 points (four goals, 13 assists) in just 14 games during the month to earn the honor. It was the third time Bedard had won the distinction, making him the first rookie to do so since Connor McDavid in 2015–16 (October, February, and March).

In the NHL's release, the league noted that Bedard had broken Brandon Saad's Blackhawks franchise record for assists in a calendar month by a rookie (Saad had 12 in March of 2013). Bedard also became the third Blackhawks rookie to record at least 17 points in a single month, joining Steve Larmer (who did it twice—19 points in 14 games in December 1982 and 17 points in 14 games in March 1983) and Jeremy Roenick (18 points in 12 games in December 1989).

In 52 games, Bedard also became the third-fastest player in Blackhawks history from the start of his NHL career to reach the 50-point mark; Bill Mosienko did it in 35 games (across three seasons from 1941–42 to 1943–44) and Terry Ruskowski in 50 games (in 1979–80). Bedard became the second 18-year-old in Blackhawks history to score 20 goals, joining only Eddie Olczyk (in 1984–85).

Bedard was held without a point five times in March; the Blackhawks were shut out in four of those games. He countered that with four multi-point games, including his five-point night against the Ducks. He finished March as the NHL rookie leader in shots on net (54), tied for first in power play points (8), second in power-play assists (7), and third in average ice time per game (21:06).

As the Blackhawks skated into UBS Arena to face the Islanders in their first game in April, Pierre LeBrun reported on TSN's "Insider Trading" segment during the broadcast that Hockey Canada had reached out to Bedard and Anaheim's Mason McTavish about participating in the World Championship, which would be held May 10–26 in Czechia.

This would be the men's tournament, a significant step up from the World Junior Championship, in which Bedard and McTavish had been stars for their country previously.

On the ice, the game started well for the Blackhawks. Almost eight minutes into the first period, Bedard and Dickinson executed a pretty passing sequence in which Dickinson played the puck around a defender off the wall to Bedard to start a rush before Bedard gave it back for the game's first goal.

Chicago took that one-goal lead into the third period, but the veteran Islanders were chasing a playoff berth and rallied in the final 20 minutes. Bo Horvat tied the game with a power play goal 93 seconds into the third and Simon Holmström scored what would be the game-winner almost eight minutes later. After a decent start, the Blackhawks were handed another loss.

Bedard was credited with four shots on goal and skated 22:52 in the game, his highest ice time total since February 21 against the Flyers. The 2–1 final score wasn't indicative of the flow of the game, however; the Islanders carried the action for most of the game and outshot the Hawks.

Many teams that were eliminated from playoff contention already would have flown home and taken the next day off; the Blackhawks had three days between games. But the team was back on the ice for a late-morning practice at Fifth Third Arena to work through some of the things that had been struggles during their 1–2–0 road trip.

The weather in Chicago was nasty for the third day in April. There was a mix of snow and rain falling outside, making it look and feel more like mid-November than a week when many kids around Chicago were on spring break. When the Hawks came out for practice, the usually filled seats above the ice were empty—with the exception of one young fan who made the trek into the city.

The Hawks had a spirited practice with some physical drills and skating. As had been the hallmark of his rookie season, Bedard stayed out on the ice with Korchinski and Kurashev as his teammates slowly left to speak with the media and leave for the afternoon. About a half hour after the rest of the team had left the ice, Korchinski and Kurashev departed to leave Bedard alone.

When he finished his extra work, Bedard skated over to the door below the bleachers and looked up to the one young fan who was there. He flipped him a puck and talked with him for a few minutes. That, too, had become part of Bedard's practice routine. Even nearing the end of his first, long NHL season, he took time to engage young fans and send them home with a souvenir. And, as was always the case, that interaction with the game's newest superstar left that fan with the biggest smile in Chicago.

When he did finally arrive in the room, Bedard was greeted with the usual collection of reporters and local television cameras. He was asked the usual questions about his game, how his shot was evolving against NHL competition, and the recent road trip. And he answered the questions with his usual amount of honesty.

He was also asked about how he felt his body was holding up with the extra work against bigger, stronger, faster players in his first NHL season. Bedard had now played in 61 games, one shy of the most regular season games he had appeared in for Regina in the WHL (during the 2021–22 season). Bedard said he felt good, once again mentioning that he works tirelessly on making sure his body is ready for the NHL grind.

He was still able to skate the heaviest minutes of any rookie forward in the NHL late in the season and put in the extra work after every practice because he valued his nutrition and recovery.

But when he was asked about the report that Hockey Canada had reached out and if he was considering playing in the World Championship a few weeks after his rookie regular season concluded, Bedard quickly said he was focused on finishing his first professional season strong. Whether or not that was something he would consider wouldn't be something he worried about while he was playing for the Chicago Blackhawks.

The Blackhawks had seven games remaining in their regular season, with the next two coming on their home ice. Chicago would host back-to-back matinee games, starting at 2:30 PM CT on both Saturday and Sunday against the Dallas Stars—who had the best record in the Western Conference at the time—and the Minnesota Wild. Both teams were well ahead of the Blackhawks in the standings and presented a strong test for their young roster.

Following their underwhelming loss at the Islanders to close their three-game trip, the Blackhawks had three days to digest their effort and plan for the Stars. Dallas was coming into the game having won eight in a row, including games against two other top Western Conference teams in the Canucks and Oilers.

To say the Blackhawks were underdogs on home ice would be an understatement.

There was a lot of buzz around the game in Chicago because the Blackhawks and NHL were trying something new with their broadcast of the game. The NHL had produced animated alternate broadcasts using characters from the popular cartoon *Big City Greens* on a national level, but had never had a fully animated broadcast of a game on a local rightsholder. The Blackhawks game against the Stars would have an alternate broadcast that was fully animated on the secondary channel of NBC Sports Chicago for this game.

The first period was physical and Blackhawks goaltender Petr Mrázek was terrific. He stood on his head as the Stars tried to take a lead and refused to allow a goal. When the Blackhawks got the game's first power play early in the second period, they made it count. Bedard scored on the advantage for his 22nd goal of his rookie season at 4:48 into the second period.

On the animated broadcast, two buckets of popcorn exploded behind the goal as Bedard's animated avatar celebrated his score. At the United Center, a young crowd was loud with its excitement. Every time Bedard scored a goal on his home ice the building lit up, but the Blackhawks marketing their early weekend games to younger fans made this afternoon's goal especially loud.

Chicago then scored again 65 seconds later and extended its lead to three less than three minutes after the second goal. Suddenly, the Blackhawks were finding ways to beat the Stars despite being outshot. Dallas was able to score a goal late in the second period, but the Blackhawks took a two-goal lead to the room.

The Stars scored late in the third period and put up a furious fight to try to tie the game in the closing minutes, but the Blackhawks held on for a 3–2 victory. Mrázek stopped 42 of 44 in the game. Bedard was credited with a team-leading four shots on net and skated 21:54 in the victory. And he did it playing primarily as a wing once again; Bedard only took two faceoffs in the game.

There wasn't much time to celebrate the win, however. Less than 24 hours after the final horn on Saturday, Bedard would have a marquee matchup on Sunday afternoon.

The Blackhawks had been rivals with the teams in Minnesota for years, first the North Stars and now, the Wild. They had faced each other in the playoffs many times. But since the Blackhawks had started their decline from the championship years, there wasn't as much juice leading up to the games.

This one would be different. Because Brock Faber was coming to Chicago.

Faber, Minnesota's rookie defenseman, was playing well enough that there was leaguewide conversation about whether he or Bedard should win the Calder Trophy as the Rookie of the Year. Faber was playing some of the heaviest minutes in the entire NHL—rookie or veteran—and was doing so very well. He was absolutely deserving of the debate.

After the Blackhawks' strong performance on Saturday, they did not show up with the same compete level for the game on Sunday. Indeed, Minnesota had them on their heels for most of the first period, but the Hawks escaped without allowing a goal.

Minnesota didn't waste much time changing that in the second period. The Wild took a lead 66 seconds into the middle frame and didn't look back. They scored three unanswered goals in the second period.

In the middle of the third period, Faber got a breakaway. He was able to draw both Blackhawks skaters who got back with him as he dropped the puck off for Kirill Kaprisov, who scored easily for his second of the game and 41st of the year.

With the assist, the Faber fans were able to make their case even stronger on social media. Bedard was held to a quiet afternoon, putting just one shot on net in just 18:54 on the ice—his lowest ice time since the Blackhawks had hosted the Red Wings on February 25.

Minnesota won 4–0 and the Blackhawks never got off the mat. The Blackhawks players were understandably disappointed with their effort in a division game. They had been playing well; Chicago had won seven of its previous 13 games. But this wasn't their afternoon.

After games on back-to-back days, the Blackhawks took the following day off to collect themselves before practicing on Tuesday in Chicago. They then flew to St. Louis for one final game against one of their most heated rivals. The last time the Blackhawks were in St. Louis, Bedard scored his "Michigan" goal, but the Blackhawks blew a late lead and took a loss the players all remembered too well.

After the disappointing loss, the Blackhawks mixed up their forward lines again. Bedard was moving back to center and Lukas Reichel was moving up to play on his wing opposite Philipp Kurashev. Richardson hoped the three could play with speed and create offense together.

The Blackhawks didn't take a morning skate in St. Louis on the day of the game and came out worse than they had against the Wild. In fact, this was just about the worst-case scenario. St. Louis scored on its first three shots of the game and the Blackhawks made a change in net; the Blues scored on the first shot after that and had a four-goal lead in the first seven minutes of the game.

Chicago was credited with one shot on net in the first 20 minutes of the game.

The Blues held a commanding 5–1 lead late in the third period when Landon Slaggert broke through and scored his first career NHL goal. There was a loud ovation from the Blackhawks bench for the former Notre Dame captain, a moment that might have been the most energy the Blackhawks showed in the entire contest.

Bedard was limited to two shots on net and was again under 20 minutes.

This loss also didn't sit well with the team. They flew back to Chicago and had a spirited practice on Thursday in preparation for hosting their final two home games of the season. Nashville, one of the hottest teams in the NHL, would be at the United Center on Friday night.

There was another new face at the practice on that Thursday. Defenseman Ethan Del Mastro, who had been an assistant captain on the gold-medal-winning Canadian team at the World Juniors with Bedard and Korchinski, was recalled earlier in the day. He was having a strong first professional season with the Blackhawks' AHL affiliate, the Rockford IceHogs, that included being named an AHL All-Star.

Del Mastro was a big defenseman who played a physical game. He had been a captain in junior and worn a letter for Canada, so he had leadership on his résumé as well; many of the Blackhawks' prospects had been either a captain or assistant captain at a prior level. Before his first NHL practice began, Del Mastro was skating on the second sheet of ice at the Blackhawks' practice facility with Korchinski and a couple coaches to go over a few things.

The Blackhawks also activated defenseman Connor Murphy off injured reserve after almost three months out of the lineup with a groin-related injury. After a long season filled with too many players spending time on IR, the Blackhawks had everyone back available to play except Taylor Hall. This was as healthy as the Blackhawks had been since the first week of the regular season.

As some of the media talked with Del Mastro in the dressing room and others with Richardson next to the ice sheet, a loud whistle was heard. The coaches were kicking Bedard off the ice. His standard extra work was being cut short on this day. Nearing the end of a long NHL season—his first as a professional—Bedard was being forced to the room.

Del Mastro's debut came on a Friday night in the Blackhawks' penultimate home game of the 2023–24 season with the playoff-bound Nashville Predators in town. Nashville had been perceived as a seller during the previous offseason; it traded center Ryan Johansen to Colorado for minimal return and bought out center Matt Duchene as its new general manager, former coach Barry Trotz, tried to fix the organization's culture. The Predators' performance was a surprise to many, and they were riding high heading into the postseason.

The success Nashville had enjoyed as it skated to a playoff berth continued at the Blackhawks' expense. The Predators scored the game's first four goals and dominated throughout. The Blackhawks were only able to generate one power play goal late in the second period, scored by Kurashev with the primary assist to Bedard. Chicago lost the game 5–1 and the effort wasn't what the players or coaches wanted.

Late in the game, Bedard found one of the other rookies—Slaggert—on his line. And when the Blackhawks had a 4-on-4 with one minute left in regulation and an offensive-zone faceoff, Chicago sent Bedard, Slaggert, Korchinski, and Del Mastro over the boards.

"I thought they had a good shift, so it was good to see," Richardson said after the game. "I think for us, that's what this time of the year is for, to take a look at that and give them some reps as well." Richardson also complimented Slaggert for being a guy who goes to the front of the net, saying the Blackhawks expect Bedard's line to put a lot of shots on net and having someone there to clean up the loose change was needed.

Chicago turned around with one day off and hosted one of the best teams in the entire NHL, the Carolina Hurricanes, in its home finale. This game came with even more excitement for Blackhawks fans. On the off day between games, the Blackhawks announced they had signed University of Michigan center Frank Nazar to his entry-level contract—and planned to play him in the final three games of the regular season.

Nazar's Michigan team had been eliminated at the Frozen Four on Thursday night. He signed on Saturday, and he was on his way to Chicago for a game on Sunday evening. He was viewed as one of the other future core pieces up front for the Blackhawks after they selected him 13th overall at the 2022 NHL Draft. Nazar scored 17 goals with 24 assists in 41 games for Michigan in his sophomore season and arrived with a lot of fans eager to see how his elite speed and skill would translate to the NHL level.

Nazar would become the sixth Blackhawks player to make his NHL debut during the 2023–24 season and took his rookie lap without a helmet, just as the previous five had before him. For all the excitement generated by his debut, the team on the other end of the rink was still playing with a chance of winning its division. Carolina was a Stanley Cup favorite and one of the better defensive teams in the entire league.

Chicago's coaches made no effort to ease Nazar into the NHL. He got run on the team's first power play—and almost scored (his shot went just over the crossbar). Ten minutes into the game, Seth Jones found him with a breakout pass and Nazar had a breakaway chance. He buried it for his first career NHL goal on his first official shot on goal. The United Center erupted.

The Blackhawks took a one-goal lead to the room after 20 minutes and were tied at one after two periods. Chicago took a 2–1 lead early in the third period on a goal from Andreas Athanasiou, but the Canes overwhelmed the Blackhawks from there. As much as Petr Mrázek could stand on his head, the better team showed it over the final 14 minutes of regulation. Three unanswered goals handed the visitors a 4–2 win to close the books on the United Center for the season.

After the game, Richardson was complimentary of Nazar's performance. He played with his signature speed and skill but also displayed a responsibility on the ice that made an impact against a very good team. For his part, Nazar spoke about the whirlwind couple days he had been through and the excitement he had to be on the ice as part of the Blackhawks' starting lineup for the national anthem and playing in an NHL game for the first time.

But it was another loss for the Blackhawks. They finished their home schedule with a 16–21–4 record on the United Center ice, which was disappointing for the players and coaches. After the game, the Blackhawks assigned Del Mastro back to their AHL affiliate, the Rockford IceHogs, to help them in their playoff run.

Chicago's final two games of the regular season stacked up to be hard tests as well. The defending Stanley Cup champion Vegas Golden Knights and Los Angeles Kings were battling for the final playoff position in the NHL; if Vegas beat the Blackhawks and Ducks in their final two games, they would win the third seed in the Pacific. If Vegas lost one of the two and the Kings won their final games, LA would be the third seed in the division. The team that didn't earn third in the Pacific would be the eighth seed in the Western Conference playoffs and get a first-round date with the Dallas Stars; the third seed would give that team a date with Connor McDavid and the Edmonton Oilers.

As was the case with Carolina, the Blackhawks were overwhelmed early by the defending champions in Vegas. But they hung around thanks to good goaltending from Mrázek once again. Trailing 2–0 late in the third period, Bedard set up Jason Dickinson for his career-best 22nd goal of the season to make the final four minutes of regulation interesting. Unfortunately, Vegas scored into the empty net to hand the Hawks a 3–1 loss.

Bedard spent most of the night on the wing again, with Dickinson handling the faceoffs on the Blackhawks' top line. He only took two faceoffs in the game and Vegas' defense stymied him the entire night. He was credited with only one shot on net in 19 minutes of ice time. With Bedard, Nazar, Slaggert, and Korchinski in the lineup, the young Blackhawks got a good, firsthand look at a championship-caliber lineup.

The Vegas win meant that Thursday, the final night of the NHL's regular season, had meaning for the LA Kings. And the Blackhawks–Kings game had the last start on the league's schedule for the entire regular season. With Vegas starting a half hour before the Blackhawks and Kings, a result from its game would have an impact on the playoffs—if the Kings won.

The Blackhawks got off to a good start with Lukas Reichel showing his speed to make a play. He scored his fifth goal of the season to give Chicago a 1–0 lead late in the first period.

The Kings had dominated the Blackhawks in their previous two meetings, however, and showed their playoff mettle in the second period. Los Angeles scored three unanswered goals in the middle stanza, and it felt like so many of the Blackhawks' road losses from a long season. Chicago was credited with only seven shots on net in 40 minutes.

After three less-than-acceptable efforts, the Blackhawks came out of the room for the third period with energy and asserted themselves. Chicago scored a power play goal early in the third period and tied the game less than 80 seconds later. When Ryan Donato scored at 6:28 into the third period, the Blackhawks had stormed to a shocking 4–3 lead. And the Blackhawks held that lead until there were 81 seconds left in the game. Phillipp Kurashev took a bad penalty late in the game and the Kings answered quickly with the advantage.

The game went to overtime, but it didn't last long in the extra session. Bedard lost the opening faceoff in overtime and Adrian Kempe took the puck, attacked the net, and scored six seconds into OT.

The Blackhawks' season came to an end with another dull thud. Chicago finished the season 7–32–2 away from the United Center, the fewest road wins in the entire NHL. Its 23–53–6 record was the worst in franchise history for a season of more than 70 games and bad enough that Chicago would own the second-best odds of winning the 2024 NHL Draft Lottery; only San Jose had a worse record. After stunning the

Dallas Stars on April 6, Chicago lost its last six games and was outscored 26–10 in those games.

"We are a team that needs to make some changes," Nick Foligno said after the final game. "This isn't good enough; this can't be good enough. This has to change drastically over the summer."

"You battle all year long with the group and you care a lot about every individual. But the reality is, when you don't win, changes are inevitable. And we understand the business side of it. We even talked about it. This might be the last time we play together—all of us, forever.

"We can't go through this again. And I certainly won't allow it. Either the mindset changes from the group or personnel changes."

While the wins and losses were a disappointment, Bedard's performance over the course of his first full professional season was still significant. He became just the third player in NHL history to lead a team in points at age 18, joining Sidney Crosby (2005–06) and Steve Yzerman (1983–84). And he did that despite missing 14 games because of his broken jaw.

Bedard's 61 points led all NHL rookies; New Jersey's Luke Hughes and Minnesota's Brock Faber (47) finished tied for second. Both appeared in all 82 games. Bedard's 22 goals led all NHL rookies; Minnesota's Marco Rossi finished with 21. Only four rookies—Bedard, Rossi, Arizona's Logan Cooley, and Philadelphia's Tyson Foerster—reached the 20-goal mark for the season. And Bedard's 39 assists were tied with Faber to lead all rookies.

Bedard also became just the seventh No. 1 overall selection since 1980–81 to lead his team in points during the season following the draft, joining Auston Matthews (2016–17), John

Tavares (2009–10), Patrick Kane (2007–08), Sidney Crosby (2005–06), Alex Ovechkin (2005–06), Mario Lemieux (1984–85), and Dale Hawerchuk (1981–82).

He also joined two individuals in making league history for a player of his age. Bedard was 18 years, 276 days old on the final day of the regular season. He became the second-youngest player in NHL history to lead rookies (outright or tied) in goals, assists, and points; only Colorado's Nathan MacKinnon (18 years, 224 days) had led all rookies at a younger age.

Bedard also became the second-youngest player in NHL history to lead his team in goals, assists, and points in a season. Only Pittsburgh's Sidney Crosby (18 years, 254 days) had led his team in all three categories at a younger age.

Chicago's flight home after the last loss was delayed, and the team got in early on Friday morning. Saturday brought the end-of-season meetings with the coaches and front office—and media. For Bedard, the morning was taking stock of a long year of facing expectations, playing through pain and frustration, and assessing his performance. His exit interview with Luke Richardson was pointed; they spoke about areas of growth and learning moments from a long season full of disappointing results.

"As good as you are, as skilled as you are, sometimes you're trying to do too much on your own," Richardson said about Bedard's mentality. "It's all good intention, because you're frustrated the team can't score, we want to do something extra here. Sometimes it just puts you and the team in a tough spot and makes it worse. I think just doing what's in your wheelhouse—with him, he's obviously an offensive guy. But knowing the game, and I think he took strides this year at times to understand the game."

"I think earlier in the year he'd be like, 'Yeah, but I could make that play.' And I'm like, 'I'm sure you can. But I don't know if the other four guys on the ice understand that you're doing that. And if you don't make that play and you're exhausted, you can't get back and defend.' So he takes it in and understands everything and he has good conversations about it. So he doesn't just like slam the stick and slam the door like a bratty teenager; he has good conversations. And I think there's a lot to learn when you're 18, no matter how good you are. And there'll still be lots to learn when you're 19 next year, but that's the league. It's the best league in the world."

Richardson pointed to Bedard's historic game in Tampa as the highlight of his season. "He was aggressive on the fore-check, aggressive on the backchecks, stole pucks, made things happen, had two goals in the game.... And then go out and do it the next night again against Florida." He also spoke at length about Bedard's improved defensive play, using his hockey sense to become a good pickpocket and create offense off his takeaways.

Blackhawks general manager Kyle Davidson added some perspective when he was asked to evaluate Bedard's season. He wasn't involved in the daily on-ice parts of Bedard's maturation, but was able to view his progress and development from his seat in the front office. With all the expectations that had been placed on Bedard coming into the league, Davidson was impressed.

"I think it was incredible," Davidson said. "I think the expectation, the weight that was put on his shoulders given his profile walking into the league, was really difficult to handle. I don't think anyone can adequately quantify the degree of difficulty of what he had to deal with off the ice to then go on to perform on the ice. We worked with him to make it as seamless as possible. And, for the most part, I think we accomplished that. But having said that, he's an 18-year-old player that had to go through more media attention than any player in recent memory, and probably more than any player entering the league ever, given the social media age that we're in right now. So I thought it was extremely impressive. And then on the ice, he certainly offensively delivered everything that you would want out of a first-year, 18-year-old player of his skill set. So I was really, really impressed."

A dozen Blackhawks skaters, some of whom were headed to an uncertain summer of free agency, met with the media that Saturday. Each spoke highly of Bedard's rookie season. Jason Dickinson said it was hard to believe Bedard was still only 18 when playing next to him—and mentioned the hope he brings for the future of the Blackhawks.

"Connor, this year, he was incredible," Dickinson said. "He's a world-class player, he's got all kinds of skill, he sees the ice incredibly well, and his future is bright. It's hard to believe he's only 18. I've got to remind myself—every day, honestly, when I see him—that he is still a kid and there's a lot of growth for him, and that his ceiling is quite high, and that there is going to be some very memorable days here in Chicago all because of that kid."

The team's de facto captain, Nick Foligno, summed up most of their thoughts effectively when he was asked about the future of the Blackhawks.

"I give that kid a ton of credit for the year he had, faced with a lot of things that were uncontrolled," Foligno said. "He seemed to just put his head down and work. We really appreciate him for that. He never really got too out of sorts with it, he just kept coming to the rink. You can tell he loves the game of hockey. And I think the biggest thing for him is just making sure he finds that joy each and every day and not getting too caught up in his expectations or other people's expectations, and just being the best version of Connor that he can be every day.

"An improved Connor Bedard is a scary thought, right?"

As always, Bedard didn't boast about his rookie marks or the elite company he had joined as an 18-year-old in the Blackhawks and NHL record books. There were ups and downs to the year, he said, and areas where he needs to grow to be a better player. He reflected on the losses and his personal performance, saying he was going to spend the summer working to get faster and be better in the defensive zone. Winning puck battles and fighting for real estate around the net were also on his list of things to improve in the coming months. Because he didn't plan on spending much time away from the rink; Bedard would represent Canada at the World Championship in Czechia and then head back home to work.

Bedard also noted that he learned a lot off the ice from the Blackhawks' veteran leaders like Foligno and Dickinson.

"Last year, I was fortunate enough to wear the C for my team in junior and I thought I got to learn a lot last year in that way and that was really good for me," he said. "But coming in, I'm 18 years old, I'm not going to be rah-rah right away and telling guys what to do or anything, but it was really good for me to just observe them and different ways to lead. Everyone's kind of got their own style and I think that's the great part about it, you ask anyone how they lead, they're going to have something different to say, so you can learn so much.

"Those guys are great, and there's a lot more that I could name that I got to just kind of observe and see different ways. And I think probably the biggest thing I learned is maybe wanting to say something, not that I was speaking up, but just when they felt the need to say something, I think that's a part of it; you don't want to be saying too much and then you're always getting mad or you always say something and it doesn't mean as much, just knowing the right time, and I thought all of our guys were really good with that."

Learning was big for Bedard. But facing the expectations of becoming the face of the franchise was another set of circumstances and requests that were at another level than Bedard had faced before in his hockey life. He felt comfortable engaging fans and being part of what the Blackhawks were doing in the community and felt that was something he wanted to do more of in the future, specifically noting some opportunities to play floor hockey with Kevin Korchinski with groups of kids in the area surrounding the United Center as a few moments he appreciated.

"That's what I want to do probably more of next year is leave a mark in the community and with the fans, and of course I want them to think of me as a great player but also someone they can connect to. In the end, we're all just normal people and I want to be a part of the community and be a positive contributor in that way and I take a lot of pride in that.... I think that's pretty special we have a platform and opportunity to do that. That's something you don't take for granted, for sure."

Even with more losses than he expected during his rookie season, Bedard was grateful to spend his rookie season with the Chicago Blackhawks.

"It's special," Bedard said. "I couldn't be more grateful for everything this year that the fans did. Right when I got drafted, there was so much support. To come into a new city, new fans, even with them kind of…. Kane and Toews were here for a long time and with them not being here this year, and [the fans] embracing us the way they did, it was incredible. We're so grateful every night that we see the United Center packed. We know it was a tough year, but the support we got throughout never wavered. We're so lucky to be in this city and be part of this franchise. It exceeded my expectations by a long way. My expectations were pretty high. I feel very fortunate."

As Bedard kept working to prepare for the World Championship in Czechia—a reality he finally confirmed now that his regular season was complete—there was one more formality on the calendar. On the final morning of April, the NHL announced the three finalists for the Calder Memorial Trophy. Bedard was joined by Minnesota defenseman Brock Faber and New Jersey defenseman Luke Hughes as the three individuals vying for the league's Rookie of the Year award.

The business side of the Blackhawks' house enjoyed strong momentum coming off Bedard's historic rookie campaign as well. The Blackhawks reported an attendance increase of 9.7 percent from the previous season, the second-largest increase in the entire NHL (the defending Eastern Conference champion Florida Panthers were up 11.7 percent from the previous year). And their average attendance of 18,836 per game ranked fourth in the NHL.

Chicago averaged 19,196 fans at weekend games (a 5.1 percent increase) and averaged 18,272 for weekday games (a 12.6 percent increase). In the weeks that followed the conclusion of the 2023–24 regular season, the Blackhawks reported a renewal rate of 96 percent on season ticket packages.

Despite winning only 23 games during Bedard's rookie season, many elements of the 2023–24 season were considered successful for the Chicago Blackhawks organization. The fans were sharing the organization's hope for a bright future around their new superstar forward.

CHAPTER 12

NOT DONE YET

O N MAY 7, THE NEXT SIGNIFICANT DATE on the NHL offseason calendar arrived. The 2024 NHL Draft Lottery was highlighted by the next star teenager heading to the presumed No. 1 pick. Boston University center Macklin Celebrini was the consensus top prospect.

The Blackhawks entered the lottery with the second-best odds of winning the top pick, better than they had the previous summer when they climbed from third to first to draft Bedard. But the odds also indicated they had a stronger likelihood of sliding back to the third or fourth overall pick than staying second.

For the first time in years, the NHL draft order didn't change. The Chicago Blackhawks stayed second in the draft, which gave the team hope for adding another difference-maker to a lineup that already included the likes of Bedard, Frank Nazar, Kevin Korchinski, Alex Vlasic, and others.

"We're really excited about how things ended up tonight," Blackhawks general manager Kyle Davidson said after the lottery. "It wasn't No. 1, but for us, the way we see this draft and what we're able to acquire at the draft in June, No. 2 is a very big win. We're really excited. I can't wait to dig in with our amateur staff next week to start the process of getting that board finalized or on the road to being finalized. Glad to know where we're picking finally.

"Winning last year and having that in our back pocket made this year a little bit easier to navigate. To be honest, it didn't weigh on me that much. Last year, it consumed everything that I feel like we did, that we talked about. This year, it's very exciting, but it's just different. It was just so much hype going into last year and it was just a different animal, so it felt a little bit different."

Meanwhile, even though the NHL's regular season had come to a close, Bedard wasn't done playing hockey for the summer. His commitment to represent his country once again in an international tournament saw him travel overseas to play in the IIHF World Championship. And, as his first professional season had played out, he found cameras everywhere he turned.

"It's our first game and we've a lot of areas to improve [in], but you know I thought we did a pretty good job and we're focused on getting better every game."

Those were Bedard's comments to TSN after Canada won their first game of the World Championship in Czechia, which came just four days after the draft lottery. Canada beat Great Britain 4–2 to start the tournament, Bedard's first for his country at the major level. After enjoying a great deal of success—historic production and back-to-back gold medals—for Canada at the World Juniors previously, Bedard was now playing in the men's format with rosters made up of seasoned professionals. And he was doing it without the bubble attached to his helmet that he'd worn since breaking his jaw in January.

The ages of the competition didn't matter; the production was there once again for the phenom. He scored two of Canada's four goals in the first game and was named Canada's player of the match. Bedard started the game on the fourth line, and his line led the offense. Bedard's two highlight-reel goals earned him recognition for the effort and a nice new Tissot watch from the IIHF.

The next day, Mother's Day, Canada was back on the ice against Denmark. Looking to add to his impressive debut, Bedard was once again the offensive leader for a Canadian team that included a handful of NHL regulars like John Tavares, Michael Bunting, and Nick Paul—who was benefiting in the box score from being on Bedard's line.

Bedard scored two more goals, both of which were instant clicks on social media, and added an assist in a resounding 5–1 win for Canada. He was the only skater on the roster with more than one point in the game, and his two goals put him on top of the tournament's leaderboard through two games with four goals already.

Even though he was the best offensive player in the game by a wide margin, Bedard did not earn player-of-the-match honors again. Blues goaltender Jordan Binnington, who stopped 19 of 20 in the win, was recognized after this game. But that didn't change the fact that Bedard was the player everyone was watching every time Canada took the ice.

Bedard was one of six Blackhawks to play in the tournament. Seth Jones and Alex Vlasic represented the United States; Lukas Reichel played for Germany (though he did not appear in their first two games); Philipp Kurashev skated for the Swiss; and Petr Mrázek was between the pipes for host Czechia.

Bedard picked up an assist in Canada's second game of the tournament, but his ice time started to dwindle as the coaches elevated other players in their rotation. Bedard scored his fifth goal of the tournament in Canada's third game, but a third-period meltdown that saw Austria score five unanswered goals to erase a 6–1 lead to force overtime led to some changes for the team.

Bedard skated only 14:30 in a 4–1 win over Norway, and he failed to register a point for the first time in the tournament. He was on the ice for only 13:19 in a 5–3 win against Finland, again without a point. In a 3–2 win against Philipp Kurashev and Switzerland, Bedard was again empty in the box score and skated just 10:14, including only two shifts in the third period.

In their final game of pool play, Bedard skated only 8:08 (10 shifts) in a game that required overtime for Canada to beat the hosts from Czechia 4–3. He was seemingly getting buried by the coaches, but Canada remained undefeated in the tournament heading to the knockout stage.

Bedard was listed as Canada's 13th forward when it posted its lineup for the quarterfinal game against Slovakia, but he was on the ice to start the game. And he came out buzzing, playing with more pace and confidence than he had in the previous few games. He picked up a pretty assist on a Nick Paul goal in the second period.

During the third period, Bedard played through a big hit attempt and created a scoring chance for a teammate in front of the net. After the goalie froze the puck, Bedard took a couple whacks from opponents and stood up for himself. Moments later after the next puck drop, Bedard was called for a questionable unsportsmanlike conduct penalty. TSN showed his father shaking his head in the stands as Bedard joined two other Canadian skaters in the penalty box.

Canada won the game 6–3 and advanced to the semifinals. Bedard was once again visible on every shift and creating offense for his team.

Bedard's ice time continued to be a focus for media at the tournament and across the Atlantic Ocean, even though Canada was playing well and advancing. And the questions he faced from a more international media field were wide-ranging, from whether he had enjoyed the bar scene in Prague to what it was like being a "wunderkind" on an international stage. When asked about the pressure of being the focus of so much attention in an event like the World Championship at a young age, Bedard offered some perspective.

"If you had asked me that a couple years ago, maybe it's different," Bedard said. "I'm grown up now. It's not really the same as much anymore. I'm just playing hockey and just kind of living my life. I'm not too worried about any of it."

But he did have to worry about more pointed questions as his ice time continued to be a focus for the media. One reporter asked Bedard if he was truly enjoying his time in the tournament, and he was more pointed with this response.

"Hockey? I enjoy hockey," Bedard said. "I don't enjoy answering these questions as much. I enjoy the game, for sure."

His ice time increased in Canada's semifinal game against Switzerland, which scratched his Chicago linemate Philipp Kurashev from the game. He picked up a pretty assist on John Tavares' game-tying goal in the third period and was the only Canadian to convert in the shootout, but the Swiss skated away with a 3–2 victory. His father was at the tournament and

TSN showed him on the screen pumping his fist after Bedard's shootout attempt was true.

Bedard's ice time was limited to only 10 minutes in the bronze medal game, which Canada lost to Sweden. After the game, Bedard was seen being less accepting of a camera following him off the ice; he put his glove in front of the camera as he followed his teammates from the ice. He hates losing, and not leaving Czechia with a medal wasn't a pleasant experience for Bedard.

The loss was the end of a long hockey season. Bedard appeared in 10 games for Canada in Europe after his first full NHL season. And whether it was in New York before the NHL season began or in Prague during the World Championship, cameras had followed him everywhere since his name was called by Blackhawks general manager Kyle Davidson in Nashville to begin the 2023 NHL Draft.

After Switzerland finished with a silver medal in the World Championship, Philipp Kurashev spoke with the *Tages-Anzeiger*, a leading Swiss newspaper based in Zürich. And, of course, playing with Bedard came up.

"Sometimes I felt sorry for him," Kurashev told the *Tages-Anzeiger*. "He was our player who had to talk to the media the most often. When it had to do with our team, he was always referred to. He had constant appointments—interviews, photoshoots, and what else I don't even know. Even in the hotels or on the street: everyone always wanted something from him."

While the long season had come to an end on the ice for Bedard, there was still the matter of flying to Las Vegas for the 2024 NHL Awards ceremony and the 2024 NHL Draft. Bedard was considered the front-runner for the Calder Memorial Trophy as the league's Rookie of the Year, but there was enough debate surrounding the candidacy of Minnesota Wild defenseman Brock Faber that the voting tally from the Professional Hockey Writers Association was at least intriguing.

"He's a great player," Bedard said about Faber at the NHL Awards. "There are so many great guys in the rookie class that could've gotten this. He was, all year, just a rock for them and what he did not only offensively but his all-around game was remarkable. He's going to be a fun guy to watch for a lot of years."

Bedard won the award, making him the first Blackhawks player to earn the Calder Trophy since Artemi Panarin following the 2015–16 season. He joined Mike Karakas, Cully Dahlstrom, Ed Litzenberger, Bill Hay, Tony Esposito, Steve Larmer, Ed Belfour, Patrick Kane—the only other No. 1 overall pick in team history—and Panarin in representing the Blackhawks as Rookie of the Year.

Bedard received 152 of 194 first-place votes from the PHWA, with the other 42 going to Faber. Thirty-nine writers listed Bedard second on their ballot, and three ranked him third in the class.

He was also named to the All-Rookie team, joining Faber and his Wild teammate forward Marco Rossi, Arizona (now Utah) forward Logan Cooley, New Jersey Devils defenseman Luke Hughes, and Carolina Hurricanes goaltender Pyotr Kochetkov. Bedard added one more "youngest" to his list for the season—he became the youngest player in Blackhawks franchise history and the 11th youngest in NHL history to earn a spot on the All-Rookie Team. He also became the 14th Blackhawks player and first since Dominik Kubalik in 2019–20 to receive All-Rookie Team honors.

"It's obviously a special year, achieving a lifelong dream of playing in the NHL, but then you just want to be with the rest of the pack and I don't want, every time I score a goal or whatever, it's a big deal because I'm the youngest kid or whatever," Bedard said after winning the Calder.

The following night, in a well-tailored red suit and black shirt, Bedard was introduced at the NHL draft—this time, not as the Blackhawks' top pick in the first round. Bedard joined owner Danny Wirtz, Davidson, and some of the Blackhawks' scouts and executives on the stage at Sphere to announce the Blackhawks' selection at No. 2 overall. Now an NHL veteran, but still an 18-year-old, Bedard introduced defenseman Artyom Levshunov to Blackhawks fans as their latest top draft pick.

As Davidson and Wirtz looked on, the moment was as symbolic for Bedard as it was for the Blackhawks franchise. There was a new teenager coming to the Windy City as a highly regarded prospect. Now Bedard was moving on to the second season of his career.

"I'm just playing hockey," Bedard said. "There's a lot of stuff that is out of your control and that's not important to me. I just want to play hockey and be with my teammates, be with your brothers every day chasing a goal."

ACKNOWLEDGMENTS

THIS BOOK WAS A SEASON-LONG PROCESS that required a great deal of collaboration and help to accomplish. So there are a lot of people I would like to thank for helping it become a reality.

First, a few folks who provided incredible stories and thoughts about Connor Bedard before and during his rookie season: Dennis Williams, Bedard's coach on Canada's 2022 and 2023 World Junior Championship teams; Brad Herauf, who coached Bedard with the Regina Pats, and Dante De Caria with the Pats as well; and chef Dee Dee Saracco, who provided tremendous insights into how Bedard managed his diet during his injury.

I do want to mention here that this past season was not an easy one for me personally. My father passed away suddenly on March 7. The support I received from the other members of the media who cover the Blackhawks on a daily basis helped keep my spirits up during an incredibly hard time. To those who sit in the United Center press box, a truly heartfelt thank you.

To my teammates and colleagues at Bleacher Nation, especially Brett Taylor and Michael Cerami, as well as Reid Rooney, for supporting me in this endeavor while I was also covering the Blackhawks for them on a daily basis, I am forever grateful.

To the members of the Blackhawks media, specifically Troy Murray and John Wiedeman, with whom I shared frequent conversations about the players on the ice (and a few hugs when my father passed), thank you for your friendship.

To the Chicago Blackhawks media relations and marketing groups, specifically Ben Fromstein, Kaylea Konoval, Chris Popovich, and Lyndsey Stroope, as well as John Steinmiller, who is now with the Chicago Cubs, thank you. And to Blackhawks general manager Kyle Davidson, who took the time to ask how I was doing, thank you as well. They were all incredibly helpful throughout this process and were also supportive after my dad passed.

Finally, and most importantly, thanks to my wife, Kristin, and my three sons—Matthew, Bobby, and Ian—for their support while I wrote this book. And to my mom, Lucette, and brother, Arthur, and his wife, Christie, who helped me keep my head up and do my best to focus on hockey during one of the hardest parts of my life, thank you for loving me. We struggled with a lot over the past months.

I wish my father, Thomas, were here to read this book. He told me frequently how much he was looking forward to the finished product. This is for you, Dad.

SOURCES

Magazines and Periodicals

The Hockey News
Tages-Anzeiger

Websites

espn.com
nhl.com
nytimes.com/athletic